WATER POLICY OVER 35 YEARS

WATER RESOURCE PLANNING, DEVELOPMENT AND MANAGEMENT

Planning and Managing of Water Resources
Peter A. Unwal (Editor)
2006. ISBN: 1-59454-757-2

Water Resources Research Progress
Liam N. Robinson (Editor)
2008. ISBN: 1-60021-973-x

Trends in Water Resources Research
Alan B. Prescott and Thomas U. Barkely (Editors)
2008. ISBN: 978-1-60456-038-1

Integrated Water Resource Management in the Kurdistan Region
Almas Heshmati
2009. ISBN: 978-1-60741-295-3

Water Quality: Physical, Chemical and Biological Characteristics
Kudret Ertuð and Ilker Mirza (Editors)
2009. ISBN: 978-1-60741-633-3

Water Infrastructure
Harald Nystroem (Editor)
2010. ISBN: 978-1-60692-479-2

Safeguarding the Nation's Drinking Water
Juan A. Schrock (Editor)
2010. ISBN: 978-1-60741-234-2

Water Policy over 35 Years
Dillon J. Sykes (Editor)
2010. ISBN: 978-1-60876-754-0

Safety and Secrecy of Bottled Water
Kelsey E. Navarro (Editor)
2010. ISBN: 978-1-60876-878-3

Water Shortages: Environmental, Economic and Social Impacts
Andrew C. Briggs (Editor)
2010. ISBN: 978-1-61728-309-3

Modeling Hydrologic Effects of Microtopographic Features
Xixi Wang (Editor)
2010. ISBN: 978-1-61668-628-4
2010. ISBN: 978-1-61668-902-5 (E-book)

Ballast Water Management: Combating Aquatic Invaders
Emily G. O'Sullivan (Editor)
2010. ISBN: 978-1-61728-000-9
2010. ISBN: 978-1-61728-232-4 (E-book)

California Water Crisis
Paula C. Serrano (Editor)
2010. ISBN: 978-1-61728-267-6
2010. ISBN: 978-1-61728-622-3 (E-book)

WATER RESOURCE PLANNING, DEVELOPMENT AND MANAGEMENT

WATER POLICY OVER 35 YEARS

DILLON J. SYKES
EDITOR

Nova Science Publishers, Inc.
New York

NOTICE TO THE READER

The Publisher has taken reasonable care in the preparation of this book, but makes no expressed or implied warranty of any kind and assumes no responsibility for any errors or omissions. No liability is assumed for incidental or consequential damages in connection with or arising out of information contained in this book. The Publisher shall not be liable for any special, consequential, or exemplary damages resulting, in whole or in part, from the readers' use of, or reliance upon, this material. Any parts of this book based on government reports are so indicated and copyright is claimed for those parts to the extent applicable to compilations of such works.

Independent verification should be sought for any data, advice or recommendations contained in this book. In addition, no responsibility is assumed by the publisher for any injury and/or damage to persons or property arising from any methods, products, instructions, ideas or otherwise contained in this publication.

This publication is designed to provide accurate and authoritative information with regard to the subject matter covered herein. It is sold with the clear understanding that the Publisher is not engaged in rendering legal or any other professional services. If legal or any other expert assistance is required, the services of a competent person should be sought. FROM A DECLARATION OF PARTICIPANTS JOINTLY ADOPTED BY A COMMITTEE OF THE AMERICAN BAR ASSOCIATION AND A COMMITTEE OF PUBLISHERS.

LIBRARY OF CONGRESS CATALOGING-IN-PUBLICATION DATA

Water policy over 35 years / editor, Dillon J. Sykes.
    p. cm.
  Includes index.
  ISBN 978-1-60876-754-0 (hardcover)
  1. Water resources development--United States--History. I. Sykes, Dillon J.
  HD1694.A5W248 2009
  333.9100973--dc22

                    2009046469

Published by Nova Science Publishers, Inc. ✦ *New York*

CONTENTS

PREFACE

The responsibility for development, management, and allocation of the nation's water resources is spread among federal, state, local, tribal and private interests. From improvements first to facilitate navigation, and later to reduce flood damages and expand irrigation in the West, the federal government has been called upon to assist with and pay for a multitude of water resource development projects. In recent decades, it also has regulated water quality, protected fish and wildlife, and facilitated water supply augmentation. Moreover, the impacts of population growth, development, and climate change are placing increasing stress on our Nation's water supplies. This book provides an overview of the set of challenges that face us in pursuit of adequate fresh water supplies, lays out the research priorities associated with those challenges and provides recommendations for a federal science to address this important issue. This book consists of public documents which have been located, gathered, combined, reformatted, and enhanced with a subject index, selectively edited and bound to provide easy access.

Chapter 1 - Concern about the availability and use of water to support the nation's people, economy, and environment has bolstered interest in establishing a national water commission. The commission structure proposed in recent legislation (e.g., H.R. 135) is similar to that of the 1968-1973 National Water Commission (NWC or Commission). As proposed in H.R. 135, the commission would assess future water demands, study current management programs, and develop recommendations for a comprehensive water strategy. Questions about a commission as an effective model and which topics a commission might consider have raised interest in assessing what the NWC recommended in its 1973 report, *Water Policies for the Future*, and how the issues that it identified have evolved.

The NWC recommended addressing the interconnection between water development and the natural environment, implementing a "users pay" or "beneficiary pays" approach, accomplishing water quality improvements, and adapting governance and organizations to meet water challenges. Since 1973, progress has been made in some of these areas; however, few actions can be traced directly to the NWC's recommendations. Nonetheless, the influence of the NWC on the evolution of water policy cannot be dismissed. Many of the problems that the Commission identified remain today, and some actions since 1973 have moved water policy toward alignment with NWC recommendations; others have moved it in the opposite direction of NWC recommendations. Shifts in institutional arrangements in general have reduced coordination of federal water agency activities and in many ways have moved away from NWC-recommended multi-objective or river basin planning. State-federal tensions over proper and respective roles continue to cloud resolution of difficult water resource issues and complicate coordination efforts.

While many support better coordination of federal water activities and a clearer national "vision" for water management, Congress has not enacted overarching water policy legislation since the 1965 Water Resources Planning Act. Instead, water policy has largely evolved through executive and judicial actions, in many cases in response to piecemeal legislation. Congress continually modifies federal water projects through amendments to existing projects and programs through Water Resources Development Acts (WRDAs), Reclamation acts, water quality legislation, and appropriations decisions. Incremental and ad hoc evolution of water policy, however, is not surprising. Water management is complicated by past decisions and investments affecting a wide range of stakeholders pursuing different goals. Specifically, federal and state laws and regulations, local ordinances, tribal treaties, contractual obligations, and economies dependent on existing water use patterns and infrastructure all affect water management. Attempts to untangle such complexities involve many constituencies with differing interests, and success is difficult to achieve. Expectations for a commission to achieve change in a complex system resistant to transformation may be unreasonable; instead, the influence of a commission may lie in how its recommendations combine with other drivers to support policy evolution.

This CRS report presents the NWC's recommendations and analyzes how issues targeted by the recommendations have evolved during the intervening years. The report focuses on key federal-level recommendations, thereby targeting what has been accomplished since 1973, what issues remain unresolved, and what additional concerns have developed.

Recent Congresses have considered legislation to establish a national water commission modeled after the 1968-1973 National Water Commission (NWC). Interest in a commission stems from basic concerns about how water is being used to support the nation's people, economy, and environment, as well as the appropriate role of the federal government in water resources management. Questions about whether a commission would be effective at addressing the nation's water resources challenges and what topics it would be charged with have raised interest in assessing the status of recommendations in the NWC's 1973 final report, *Water Policies for the Future*. In its report, the Commission made more than 200 recommendations for improving federal and state water resources actions.

As Congress considers whether to establish a new "Twenty-first Century Water Policy Commission," questions arise about the scope and effect of the 1973 NWC report. After a brief introduction to U.S. water policy and the NWC, this report presents a general summary of the NWC report, its recommendations, and how these issues have evolved since 1973. The issues are organized into five categories: (1) "Governance and Institutional Issues"; (2) "Water and the Natural Environment"; (3) ""Users Pay" or "Beneficiary Pays" Approach"; (4) "Improvements to Water Quality"; and (5) "Water Rights." The remainder of this CRS report provides greater detail on issues that fall under each of the five broad categories. The report provides an overview of key issues and recommendations identified by the NWC; it neither covers the entire NWC report nor provides an exhaustive assessment of progress made on Commission recommendations.

Chapter 2 - Water is essential to maintain human health, agriculture, industry, ecosystem integrity, and the economic vitality of communities and the Nation. Throughout history, a key measure of a civilization's success has been the degree to which human ingenuity has harnessed fresh water resources for the public good. Indeed, civilizations have failed because of their inability to provide a safe and reliable water supply in the face of changing water resources and needs.

In: Water Policy Over 35 Years
Editors: Dillon J. Sykes

ISBN: 978-1-60876-754-0
© 2010 Nova Science Publishers, Inc.

Chapter 1

35 YEARS OF WATER POLICY: THE 1973 NATIONAL WATER COMMISSION AND PRESENT CHALLENGES

Betsy A. Cody and Nicole T. Carter

SUMMARY

Concern about the availability and use of water to support the nation's people, economy, and environment has bolstered interest in establishing a national water commission. The commission structure proposed in recent legislation (e.g., H.R. 135) is similar to that of the 1968-1973 National Water Commission (NWC or Commission). As proposed in H.R. 135, the commission would assess future water demands, study current management programs, and develop recommendations for a comprehensive water strategy. Questions about a commission as an effective model and which topics a commission might consider have raised interest in assessing what the NWC recommended in its 1973 report, *Water Policies for the Future*, and how the issues that it identified have evolved.

The NWC recommended addressing the interconnection between water development and the natural environment, implementing a "users pay" or "beneficiary pays" approach, accomplishing water quality improvements, and adapting governance and organizations to meet water challenges. Since 1973, progress has been made in some of these areas; however, few actions can be traced directly to the NWC's recommendations. Nonetheless, the influence of the NWC on the evolution of water policy cannot be dismissed. Many of the problems that the Commission identified remain today, and some actions since 1973 have moved water policy toward alignment with NWC recommendations; others have moved it in the opposite direction of NWC recommendations. Shifts in institutional arrangements in general have reduced coordination of federal water agency activities and in many ways have moved away from NWC-recommended multi-objective or river basin planning. State-federal tensions over proper and respective roles continue to cloud resolution of difficult water resource issues and complicate coordination efforts.

While many support better coordination of federal water activities and a clearer national "vision" for water management, Congress has not enacted overarching water policy legislation since the 1965 Water Resources Planning Act. Instead, water policy has largely evolved through executive and judicial actions, in many cases in response to piecemeal legislation. Congress continually modifies federal water projects through amendments to existing projects and programs through Water Resources Development Acts (WRDAs), Reclamation acts, water quality legislation, and appropriations decisions. Incremental and ad hoc evolution of water policy, however, is not surprising. Water management is complicated by past decisions and investments affecting a wide range of stakeholders pursuing different goals. Specifically, federal and state laws and regulations, local ordinances, tribal treaties, contractual obligations, and economies dependent on existing water use patterns and infrastructure all affect water management. Attempts to untangle such complexities involve many constituencies with differing interests, and success is difficult to achieve. Expectations for a commission to achieve change in a complex system resistant to transformation may be unreasonable; instead, the influence of a commission may lie in how its recommendations combine with other drivers to support policy evolution.

This CRS report presents the NWC's recommendations and analyzes how issues targeted by the recommendations have evolved during the intervening years. The report focuses on key federal-level recommendations, thereby targeting what has been accomplished since 1973, what issues remain unresolved, and what additional concerns have developed.

Recent Congresses have considered legislation to establish a national water commission modeled after the 1968-1973 National Water Commission (NWC).[1] Interest in a commission stems from basic concerns about how water is being used to support the nation's people, economy, and environment, as well as the appropriate role of the federal government in water resources management. Questions about whether a commission would be effective at addressing the nation's water resources challenges and what topics it would be charged with have raised interest in assessing the status of recommendations in the NWC's 1973 final report, *Water Policies for the Future*.[2] In its report, the Commission made more than 200 recommendations for improving federal and state water resources actions.

As Congress considers whether to establish a new "Twenty-first Century Water Policy Commission," questions arise about the scope and effect of the 1973 NWC report. After a brief introduction to U.S. water policy and the NWC, this report presents a general summary of the NWC report, its recommendations, and how these issues have evolved since 1973. The issues are organized into five categories: (1) "Governance and Institutional Issues"; (2) "Water and the Natural Environment"; (3) ""Users Pay" or "Beneficiary Pays" Approach"; (4) "Improvements to Water Quality"; and (5) "Water Rights." The remainder of this CRS report provides greater detail on issues that fall under each of the five broad categories. The report provides an overview of key issues and recommendations identified by the NWC; it neither covers the entire NWC report nor provides an exhaustive assessment of progress made on Commission recommendations.[3]

U.S. WATER POLICY AND THE 1968-1973 NATIONAL WATER COMMISSION: AN INTRODUCTION

Water Management Roles in a Federalist System

The responsibility for development, management, and allocation of the nation's water resources is spread among federal, state, local, tribal, and private interests. The federal government has been involved in water resources development since the earliest days of the nation. From improvements first to facilitate navigation, and later to reduce flood damages and expand irrigation in the West, the federal government has been called upon to assist with and pay for a multitude of water resource development projects. In recent decades, it also has regulated water quality, protected fish and wildlife, and facilitated water supply augmentation. However, the federal role also has limits. For example, Congress has generally deferred to the states' primacy in intrastate water allocation.[4] While local municipalities have largely been responsible for developing and distributing water supplies, the federal government in limited cases also has been authorized to assist communities with water supply development. Land use planning and zoning are almost always within the purview of local governments; however, federal and state actions and interests may run counter to local interests and actions, and vice versa.

Water Policy Challenges in a Federalist System

Nearly two centuries of water resource project development, environmental and resource management activities, and population shifts have resulted in a complex web of federal and state laws and regulations, local ordinances, tribal treaties, contractual obligations, and economies based on existing water use patterns and infrastructure. These laws have been enacted for diverse purposes, including to allocate, manage, and regulate water use, protect its quality, develop its energy potential, contain its destructive powers, and restore or maintain its biological integrity.

Development of these laws has required the action of numerous congressional committees and federal agencies. At the congressional level, this interest has resulted in a set of diverse and sometimes overlapping committee jurisdictions dealing with various aspects of water policy.[5] At the executive branch level, this interest and congressional direction has resulted in many agencies and organizations being involved in different but related aspects of federal water policy. This dispersed arrangement complicates management of large river systems (e.g. Missouri, Mississippi, Columbia, and Colorado River basins) and estuaries (e.g. Chesapeake Bay and the San Francisco Bay and Sacramento-San Joaquin Rivers Delta (California Bay-Delta)), especially where anadromous fisheries or threatened or endangered species are involved. For example, fishes navigating some of these large river systems must pass through waters and facilities managed by multiple state and federal agencies and are affected by state, federal, local, and tribal water and land management decisions.

Multiple laws and responsibilities also confuse entities looking for assistance with local water projects or other related activities, as well as those seeking to increase recreational opportunities, fish and wildlife protection, and scenic enjoyment. For example, multiple federal programs exist to help communities with rural water supply, wastewater treatment, drinking water quality, and other water-related needs.

At the state level, concern arises any time the federal government is perceived to be infringing on the concept of state primacy in water allocation or controlling water management decisions. This federal-state tension is mirrored in executive-legislative tensions over water resources development and management. Thus, in responding to the former concern, many experts have called for a "national" (i.e., not federal) commission or other mechanism that would involve states and localities in development of a national water policy "vision."[6]

Complicating matters further is the dynamic nature of water itself. The basic hydrologic cycle, climate variability—including floods and droughts— and the chemical, physical, and biological nature of surface and ground waters are in a constant state of flux.

Criticism of the fractured nature of federal water policy has been a recurrent theme for decades. Historically, countless commissions, councils, and studies have called for new directions in water policy and better planning, evaluation, and coordination of federal actions.[7] Options used in the past have included formal and informal coordination entities within the executive branch, non-governmental commissions tasked with reviewing past policies and laws, and a legislative branch committee made up of key committee leaders.

Congress has not enacted any comprehensive—or overarching—change in federal water resources management or national water policy since enactment of the 1965 Water Resources Planning Act (P.L. 89-80; 42 U.S.C. § 1962). The Water Resources Planning Act was the direct result of recommendations of the Senate Select Committee on National Water Resources, a congressional committee established to review national water resources policy.[8] Although an assessment of the nation's water resource *conditions* was last conducted in 1975 and several entities have studied selected aspects of water policy and management, the last systematic and comprehensive review of nationwide federal water *policy* was the 1973 NWC report. Congress, which represents local interests, often has reacted to proposals to change or reorganize water organizations and institutions as attempts to exert federal control over state and local matters or as attempts to concentrate power and decision-making in the executive branch.

Congress arguably has been comprehensive (in the aggregate) in its approach to legislating on many different aspects of water law and policy, but it has not done so in a coordinated or overarching way. Any attempt to untangle the complexities of current water policy involves many constituencies with differing interests, and becomes politically difficult to sustain. Instead of comprehensive or overarching legislation, Congress has enacted numerous incremental changes, agency by agency, statute by statute. Both the executive and judicial branches have responded to these changes and, over time, have developed policy and planning mechanisms largely on an ad hoc basis. When coordination of federal activity has occurred, it has been driven largely by pending crises, such as potential threatened or endangered species listings, droughts, floods, and hurricanes; and by local or regional initiatives. Concern about water supply and its development, however, has bolstered recent interest in legislation to establish a national water commission to assess future water demands, study current management programs, and develop recommendations for a comprehensive strategy.

Genesis of the National Water Commission

The National Water Commission was created by Congress in 1968 to "provide for a comprehensive review of national water resource problems and programs ... "[9] Congress specifically tasked the Commission to (1) review present and anticipated national water resource problems, including making projections of water "requirements" and alternative ways of meeting such requirements, giving consideration to a host of interests and technological approaches; (2) consider economic and social consequences of water resource development; and (3) advise on such specific water resource matters as might be referred to it by the President and the then- existing Water Resources Council (WRC).[10] (See box, "Brief History of the Water Resources Council.")

Creation of the Commission stemmed largely from congressional debate over development of dams and related irrigation infrastructure in the Lower Colorado River Basin, which in total "would use more water than the river could supply."[11] Members of Congress from the Pacific Northwest, including the chairman of the Senate Interior and Insular Affairs Committee, objected to proposals to transfer water from the Columbia River Basin to supply the needs of states in the Southwest, and a political compromise was reached to create a commission to study water resource problems—a suggestion originally proposed by the Bureau of the Budget.[12] Passage of legislation authorizing the National Water Commission was a direct result. The Commission was made up of seven members appointed by the President.[13] Although none was allowed to be a federal employee, some, including chairman Charles F. Luce, had formerly held senior positions in the federal government. Members were chosen largely for their expertise in a variety of fields related to water resource management. Together, they represented a range of geographic regions and backgrounds in government, industry, and law.[14] Unlike the common practice of today, no special interests were required to be represented.

Response to the National Water Commission

While progress has been made on addressing many of the problems identified by the Commission, particularly through successive enactment of many Water Resource Development Acts, Reclamation laws, and amendments to water quality legislation, few actions can be directly traced to the Commission's 1973 recommendations. Aside from immediate oversight hearings by the Senate Interior and Insular Affairs Committee and Senate Public Works Committee, and references in appropriations hearings, the report received no direct follow-up action. In 1978, the Commission's executive director, Theodore Schad, noted that the report had remained in "limbo," awaiting mandated action from the WRC and final transmission from the President to the Congress.[15] Schad went on to note:

> It appears these actions [WRC comments and recommendations from the President to Congress] will never be taken. President Nixon became preoccupied with his defense against the Watergate scandals which ultimately led to his resignation. The Ford administration occupied itself with the Section 80 study of water policy. And the Carter administration appears to have accepted Santayana's comment as its precept [that "those who cannot remember the past are condemned to repeat it"].[16]

Instead of direct action to implement the Commission's recommendations, it appears that water policy has continued to evolve—in some areas, much as the Commission predicted—and that this evolution has had many drivers, including but not limited to the Commission findings. For example, a shift from federal grants to loans for local water quality activities is consistent with the Commission's recommendation for an end to such grants; however, the change was not a direct response to the Commission's recommendations. Changes in Reclamation law in 1982 and federal cost-share policies in 1986 also reflected Commission recommendations. Again, however, it is doubtful that these changes were a direct response to Commission recommendations; rather, they reflect the culmination of many forces to bring about change.

Despite the evolution in water policy, many of the problems identified by the Commission remain today. Often, what makes these problems so intractable is the difficulty in reaching agreement among varied stakeholders as to the proper and respective roles and responsibilities of federal, state, local, tribal, and nongovernmental entities in water management and the distinct dichotomy between agencies, institutions, and constituencies dealing with various aspects of water resource issues on the one hand and water quality issues on the other. Whether a new commission could succeed in promoting direct responses where others have found difficulty is uncertain. Expectations for a commission to directly achieve changes in a complex system resistant to transformation may be unreasonable; instead, the influence of a commission may lie in how its recommendations combine with other drivers to create support for an evolution in policy.

SUMMARY OF THE COMMISSION'S 1973 REPORT AND ITS RECOMMENDATIONS

In June 1973, the National Water Commission completed its five-year term and published its final report, *Water Policies for the Future*. The Commission found that many of the country's water policies were based on outdated goals and objectives (e.g., settlement of the West, territorial expansion of navigation) and on flawed assumptions about future water needs. The Commission viewed itself as being at the cusp of a shift in water resources management, as the era of large dam construction and other large-scale development investments tapered off; this put the Commission in a unique position to take stock of past policies, assess implementation of then-current programs, and make recommendations for future federal, state, and local policies in water resource and water quality management. The report was based on hundreds of documents, special studies contracted by the Commission, eight public hearings, and other meetings conducted since its inception in 1968. Early chapters of the report describe the long history of water resource development and federal activities related to water supply and water quality, as well as water demand projections.

General Themes of Recommendations

The final Commission report included 17 chapters and supporting appendixes and 232 recommendations. It articulated seven basic themes, which together provided the foundation for the Commission's conclusions and recommendations:[17]

- The demand for water in the future is not predetermined and does not follow an inexorable growth pattern, but depends on policy decisions that society controls.
- A change in emphasis from water development to preservation and enhancement of water quality and environmental preservation is underway and will continue into the future.
- Water development planning must be tied more closely to water quality planning, and all water planning to land use planning.
- Meeting future demands necessitates conservation, increased efficiency, and better use of water for agriculture, industry, and domestic and municipal purposes.
- Sound economic principles, such as consumers' willingness to pay, should be used to encourage better use of water resources, but tempered by governmental attention to protection of environmental values.
- Updated laws and legal institutions are needed to implement future water policies.
- The level of government (federal, regional, state, or local) nearest the water resource problem and capable of adequately representing all interests should control water resource development, management, and protection.

In analyzing the above themes, the text of the report, historical analysis of the Commission's work, and congressional statements and hearings following the release of the 1973 report, CRS has identified several broad issues areas: a need for reevaluation of federal project planning and evaluation, as well as relationships among federal, state, local and tribal entities with respect to water management and water rights; concern about the effects of water resources management on the natural environment; a movement toward recovering from direct beneficiaries the costs of federal investments in water projects; and concern over degraded water quality. These issues are summarized in the following five sections: (1) "Governance and Institutional

Issues"; (2) "Water and the Natural Environment"; (3) ""Users Pay" or
"Beneficiary Pays" Approach"; (4) "Improvements to Water Quality"; and (5)
"Water Rights."

Governance and Institutional Issues

A fundamental and overarching issue area addressed by the NWC was
governance and related institutional mechanisms to address water management
and planning. In particular, the Commission recommended numerous changes
to the institutional structure through which water resources actions were
planned, evaluated, and managed. Specific governance and institutional topics
covered by the Commission included (1) water resources project planning and
evaluation; (2) accounting for the environment in project development; (3)
public participation in water resources planning; (4) federal water resources
coordination; and (5) water resources authorizations, budgets, and
appropriations. Although the basic functioning of the authorization, budgeting,
and appropriations processes for water resources has not changed significantly
since 1973, a few major changes in organizations and focus have altered the
institutional landscape affecting water resources management. These include
disbandment of the executive-level Water Resources Council (WRC) and most
of the federal river basin commissions, and increased emphasis on state
responsibility for water management and development. These changes largely
moved water resources planning and evaluation in the opposite direction from
Commission recommendations. (See box, "Brief History of the Water
Resources Council.")

The Commission also predicted (accurately) that large-scale federal
development would play a less significant role than in the past,[18] and instead
identified joint or coordinated management of multipurpose water facilities,
water quality, and local and nonfederal uses as more pressing. The predictions
of less large-scale development and the increasing challenges of managing
rivers for multiple uses have largely come to fruition. While the federal
government has constructed many multipurpose projects, multi-objective
federal planning—that is, planning for multiple objectives such as national and
regional economic development, environmental quality, and other social and
safety concerns—has not been implemented widely or consistently since the
mid-1980s. The 1983 federal water resources planning guidance moved away
from the 1970s planning guidance of multi-objective planning, and reverted to
a focus on national economic development. This 1983 guidance remains in

effect,[19] although Congress recently enacted legislation requiring its update.[20] Notwithstanding the current planning guidance's focus on economic criteria, the environment has received greater attention in federal water resources project planning and operations, due in large part to implementation of environmental laws, in particular the National Environmental Policy Act (NEPA; P.L. 91-190, 42 U.S.C. §4321 et seq.) and the Endangered Species Act (ESA; P.L. 93-205, as amended; 16 U.S.C. §§ 1531-1543).

The Commission found that budgeting procedures neither reflected nor promoted regional or long-term water resources development, and projects were often presented to Congress and considered individually. Considering project authorizations and appropriations as part of comprehensive river basin and regional development plans, as recommended by the Commission, has not been an option since the early 1980s, when most larger-scale federal water resources planning efforts were halted. Budgeting for the two largest federal water resource agencies (the Corps and the Bureau of Reclamation) also has remained largely project-specific, while federal funding for water quality infrastructure is largely done via formula-based funding to state revolving fund programs.

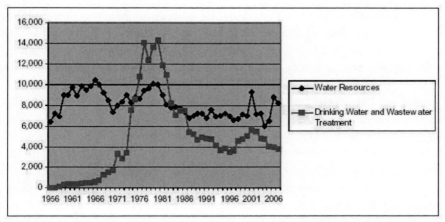

Source: CRS, with data from the Congressional Budget Office, CBO Infrastructure Spending Supplemental Tables, 2008 Update, available at http://www.cbo.gov/doc.cfm?index=9135.

Figure 1. Federal Water Resources and Water Quality Spending (1956-2007 in millions of 2006 dollars)

In terms of federal appropriations for water programs, a shift from development to preservation indeed occurred; where once water resource development was predominant in water program spending, federal water quality spending significantly increased in the 1970s and has remained well above pre-1970s levels, while water resources development spending has experienced a modest decline (see **Figure 1**). With regard to water resources program focus, development has slowed and federal water resource agencies now must take into account the environment in planning, constructing, and operating projects. Still, the degree to which development and environmental protection are evaluated and weighted remains central to many current water resources conflicts.

Water and the Natural Environment

The Commission found that by 1973, the best sites for dams and other water resource development projects had been used, that many projects had heavily affected the environment, and that the public had turned its support from development to environmental and water quality preservation. The Commission recommended a similar shift from development (construction of dams, irrigation ditches, channels, etc.) toward preservation and improvement of water quality. Its recommendations ranged across numerous fields, including (1) reservoir development; (2) flood policy; (3) estuaries and the coastal zone; (4) channelization; and (5) fish and wildlife protection.

Many of the water and natural environment concerns raised by the NWC have been addressed via implementation of environmental laws at their infancy in 1973—for example NEPA, ESA, and the Clean Water Act (P.L. 92-500; 33 U.S.C. § 1251 et seq.). Further, many of the largest current federal water actions are attempting to address environmental or species concerns through ecosystem restoration and stream rehabilitation (e.g., Everglades restoration, San Joaquin River restoration, and San Francisco Bay/San Joaquin River and Sacramento Delta (Bay-Delta) restoration); whether these recent efforts will perform as planned and whether the federal-nonfederal collaboration central to many of them will function effectively and efficiently remains in question. As a consequence, whether these changes and efforts **adequately address the Commission's concerns is a matter of disagreement.**

"Users Pay" or "Beneficiary Pays" Approach

The Commission also supported greater application of "users pay" and "beneficiary pays" approaches, which are founded on the concept that those directly benefitting from federal investment ought to pay the for investment. The twin goals of this approach were to improve *equity* and *efficiency*. These goals were the focus of several chapters in the final report, and the users pay and beneficiary pays policies were woven throughout the report. The Commission focused on (1) increasing (or establishing) general nonfederal cost shares of projects by federal water resource agencies (e.g., the Corps of Engineers and the Bureau of Reclamation); (2) establishing inland waterway user charges; (3) changing federal irrigation policy and implementing reforms to the Reclamation program (i.e., reducing federal irrigation subsidies and complexities); and (4) addressing appropriate pricing of water and wastewater services.

At congressional hearings, the Commission stated that heavy federal investment in water resources development made sense in the early part of the nation's history and through the first half of the 20th century, but changing federal priorities necessitated changes in water policies. The needed changes included improving cost recovery and eliminating program duplication and cross-purpose policies.

Cost recovery remains part of the ongoing discussions of the proper federal role in water policy. For example, ongoing tensions between successive administrations and recent congresses over funding for federally supported water reuse and rural water projects have revolved mostly around what the proper federal role is in financing local municipal and industrial water supply projects. Federal program duplication also generates federal investment concerns; on the other hand, congressional supporters often justify new projects and programs as fulfilling an unmet social purpose. Regarding costly cross-purpose programs, numerous studies since 1973 have questioned the incentives created by federal assistance for flood damage reduction infrastructure (like levees and floodwalls). Specifically, if this infrastructure encourages commercial, residential, and industrial development in floodplains, the social and economic costs are generally greater when flooding occurs.

Increasing or changing nonfederal cost shares or establishing special fees for beneficiaries of water projects consistently proves politically difficult.[21] Nonetheless, some progress has been made in addressing the Commission's recommendations related to containing costs—most notably through increased cost shares for certain port development, flood projects, and establishment of a barge fuel tax. Some economists, however, argue that these steps have been insufficient to address the full range of inefficient cost share and water pricing policies.

Improvements to Water Quality

The elements of the final report that addressed water pollution control were some of the most controversial,[22] chiefly because the Commission rejected some key concepts that Congress had recently adopted in the Federal Water Pollution Control Act Amendments of 1972 (P.L. 92-500; 33 U.S.C. § 1251 et seq., commonly referred to as the Clean Water Act (CWA)). The draft final report was released one month after enactment of that major law, and the final report barely eight months after enactment. The Commission rejected the zero discharge goal and the core regulatory approach central to the CWA.

The CWA is viewed today as one of the most successful environmental laws in terms of achieving its statutory goals, and the CWA programs have been widely supported by the public. The Commission made observations that remain valid about the extent of water pollution problems, despite water quality improvements that have occurred since then. Issues on which the Commission focused some recommendations, such as planning, federal and state roles, and enforcement through discharge permits, have been and remain basic elements of implementing water quality programs. The need to adequately fund pollution control activities, highlighted in several recommendations, also remains a challenge for policymakers.

Water Rights

The Commission also focused on the scarcity of water as a resource and adapting to more efficient use and allocation. It suggested that procedural mechanisms and legal regulations, including adjustments to water rights, be implemented to ensure that water was used efficiently and effectively. Congress has enacted legislation protecting social and noneconomic values while respecting the state-based water rights frameworks; many states also have modified their water rights systems to protect social values. The Commission described water supply in the West as limited and near full appropriation, and it framed the Indian water rights issue as a conflict in the West between Indian rights to water and water development, on the one hand, and the potential harm to extensive non-Indian water development and use, on the other. As is the case today, Indian water rights claims were largely unquantified. The Commission found that resultant uncertainties created an urgent need to resolve Indian water rights claims; many perceive this as still being the case.

ANALYSIS OF THE 1973 NWC RECOMMENDATIONS

The following sections provide an overview and analysis of the Commission's recommendations. Each section includes a brief discussion of issues identified by the Commission, a listing of key recommendations, and a discussion of whether certain recommendations have been implemented. In many cases, a discussion of how issues identified may have evolved is also included.

GOVERNANCE AND INSTITUTIONAL ISSUES

The Commission found that future water requirements could not be fully assessed without taking into account how water resources are governed and what institutional structures guide their management, use, and allocation. The Commission emphasized that policy choices would greatly influence future water use and water "needs" or "requirements"—that future water "demands" would depend on multiple factors and future polices.

> A persistent tendency of water resources planning has been the issuance of single valued projections of water use into the future under a continuation of present policies, leading to astronomical estimates of future water requirements.... The amount of water that is actually used in the future will depend in large measure on public policies that are adopted. The National Water Commission is convinced that there are few water "requirements.".... But there are "demands" for water and water-related services that are affected by a whole host of other factors and policy decisions, some in fields far removed from what is generally considered to be water policy.[23]

With regard to government programs and institutions affecting water policy, the Commission made many recommendations related to (1) water resources project planning and evaluation; (2) accounting for the environment in project development; (3) public participation in water resources planning; (4) federal water resources coordination; and (5) water resources authorization, budget and appropriations.

Water Resources Project Planning and Evaluation[24]

Issue

The NWC predicted a less significant role for large-scale federal project development (e.g. construction of locks, dams, levees, and diversion facilities) than in the past. The Commission instead identified joint or coordinated management of multipurpose water facilities, water quality, and local and nonfederal uses as more pressing. It concluded that comparisons of alternative water uses would become increasingly important as demands increased on limited supplies. The Commission believed that estimating the values of various uses and pricing policies would be important to achieve efficient water allocation. It concluded that federal investment in water resources projects was inefficient for achieving regional economic development, and cautioned that careful development and assessment of project proposals were necessary to enhance their effectiveness and offset losses in other regions.

The Commission found water resource project planning insufficient in its integration with land-use planning, water quality and environmental concerns, and the interests of the general public. The Commission criticized large river basin and watershed plans as avoiding needed prioritization, being unrealistically ambitious, and failing to capture the issues significant to metropolitan areas. It noted that important non-quantitative issues and judgments were buried in the analysis of some plans, and that federal planning requirements for states were costly while producing unclear state benefits.

The Commission supported broadening traditional objectives of water resources plans, but was uncertain how to properly evaluate multi-objective plans and their alternatives. The Commission determined that society was not only concerned with national economic consequences, but also with water projects' nonmarket and regional effects. It found that a bias toward construction projects and projects within agency mission areas resulted in inappropriately narrow alternative formulation during the early phases of planning. In particular, the Commission found that there was a bias against alternatives for no action, delayed investments, and nonstructural measures (e.g., pricing, metering, conservation, evacuation, floodproofing). It found that the evaluation of alternatives seldom adequately treated adverse, indirect, social, and non-monetized effects. The Commission commented on the bias caused by the dominance of benefit-cost analyses in evaluation and selection, in particular the often overriding weight given the benefit-cost ratio in identifying the preferred alternative.

The Commission also identified municipal water supply and wastewater treatment; recreation use; water quality and pollution control; and power plant siting and licensing as significant planning challenges. The Commission's planning recommendations focused on these issues as they relate to water resources planning. The discussion below similarly focuses on water resources planning, rather than water quality and other planning issues.

NWC Recommendations
To improve planning, the Commission recommended:

- integrating land-use and water planning at the state, federal, and local levels, and in coordinating institutions such as river basin commissions;
- increasing federal funds for state water planning, and access to these funds by local and interstate planning entities;
- authorizing federal-state-local planning organizations if there is a federal interest, and giving more intensive and continued attention to water management needs of smaller basins and metropolitan areas;
- estimating values for alternative water uses as part of basin plans, as appropriate;
- analyzing water resources as hydrologic systems (i.e., accounting for quantity, quality, timing, resource location, and subsequent uses); and
- judging fish, wildlife, and aesthetic values indirectly (i.e., not by economic evaluation), and basing decisions on the value of uses preserved exceeding the value of the uses foregone.

For evaluating alternatives, the Commission recommended:

- approving the multi-objective planning approach in the WRC's (then-proposed) Principles and Standards for water resources planning;
- not relying solely on benefit-cost analysis for decision-making;

- determining nonfederal sponsors' willingness to pay for a project, and to consider that a measure of its attractiveness as an investment; and
- basing the discount rate for projects on average yield rates for long-term Treasury obligations.

Current Status and Implementation

Significant shifts have occurred in water resources planning since 1973. In the early 1970s, water resource agency planning Principles and Standards incorporated environmental, regional, and social effects, as well as national economic development factors.[25] Consistent with the Commission's recommendations, the WRC revised the Principles and Standards. New, extensive Principles and Standards were published under the Carter Administration in 1979. Soon thereafter, the Reagan Administration replaced this guidance with the "Principles and Guidelines" just as the WRC disbanded in 1983, which revised the Principles to focus decision-making on economic criteria but left out the analytic provisions.[26]

The Principles and Guidelines moved away from the 1970s Principal and Standards' use of a multi-objective planning and evaluation framework, thus reverting back to a focus on national economic development. As the Commission envisioned, regional development and resource development projects continued their decline after 1973. Much of the post-Commission federal planning has been concentrated at the Corps and at a smaller scale in USDA watershed programs. In the early 1980s, President Reagan also dissolved the majority of the large-scale river basin commissions.

As with other areas addressed by the Commission, the advent of new environmental laws (e.g., NEPA and ESA) has also significantly shaped federal water resources planning since 1973. (See "Accounting for the Environment in Project Development" and "Public Participation in Water Resources Planning" for more information.)

BRIEF HISTORY OF THE WATER RESOURCES COUNCIL

U.S. water resource agencies largely acted autonomously in proposing project plans until an interagency Water Resources Council was established in 1965 to coordinate federal water programs and policy. The Council was created by the Water Resources Planning Act of 1965 (P.L. 89-80); it challenged more established institutional decision mechanisms of both executive and legislative branches and was subsequently disbanded in

1983. The 1965 act declares that "the policy of the Congress is to encourage the conservation, development, and utilization of water and related land resources of the United States on a comprehensive and coordinated basis by the Federal Government, States, localities, and private enterprise ..." Specific duties given the Council were to:

- conduct continuing "assessments" of water supplies;
- coordinate basin plans with larger regional and federal programs, including making policy recommendations;
- establish "principles and standards" for evaluating projects, i.e., integrating environmental and social objectives with cost-benefit analysis;
- review and make recommendations on basin commission plans; and
- allot financial grants to states for planning assistance.

Council Activities, 1968-1978

With 50 professional staff, the Council issued unprecedented and highly detailed national water assessments in 1968 and in 1975. Dozens of river basin studies and major planning studies were completed, as was issuance of new principles and standards for project evaluation.

The Council operated in an environment dominated by a few large water project construction agencies and the legislative committees of jurisdiction. Although the Council operated as a sub-Cabinet (staff-level) committee, it was nominally made up of the Secretaries of Agriculture, Army, Health, Interior, and Transportation and the (then) Federal Power Commission chairman; later the Housing Secretary and Administrator of the Environmental Protection Agency were named as associate members, while "observers" included the Office of Management and Budget, Council on Environmental Quality, Tennessee Valley Authority, and river basin commission chairpersons.

In 1978, the Carter Administration initiated an effort to reform federal water policy—initially employing a "hit list" of about 20 large water projects for which de-authorization was sought. The Council was called upon to assist in the effort, and Council staff were used to independently review the water agencies' project justifications. Eventually, congressional funding provisions maintained many projects and prohibited the Council's independent reviews.

Early 1980s

In early 1981, Interior Secretary James Watt, serving as Council chairman, requested reduced Council funding. The action was consistent with the Reagan Administration's outlook that states should play a more active role in water policy activities. All the organizational and staff planning functions of the Council and basin commissions were disbanded, and a revised set of "Principles and Guidelines" were issued in 1983 as one of the last formal actions of the Council. Although the Water Resources Planning Act has not been repealed and thus authorization of the Council remains statutorily, no funding for the Council has been appropriated since FY1983.

Prepared by Betsy A. Cody and H. Stephen Hughes

Planning and Evaluation Guidance

The 1983 Principles and Guidelines remain in effect. How they focus planning, evaluation, and selection of the preferred federal project alternative on national economic benefits (NED) has been widely criticized, particularly as interest and support for aquatic ecosystem restoration and environmental protection has grown. Furthermore, Hurricane Katrina drew national attention to concerns about the incorporation of public safety in planning. In a Water Resources Development Act of 2007 (WRDA 2007, P.L. 110-114) provision, Congress called for the Secretary of the Army to update the Principles and Guidelines by the end of 2009. The same provision also stated a national water resources planning policy.[27]

It is the policy of the United States that all water resources projects should reflect national priorities, encourage economic development, and protect the environment by—(1) seeking to maximize sustainable economic development; (2) seeking to avoid the unwise use of floodplains and flood-prone areas and minimizing adverse impacts and vulnerabilities in any case in which a floodplain or flood-prone area must be used; and (3) protecting and restoring the functions of natural systems and mitigating any unavoidable damage to natural systems.

How this provision is implemented (i.e., how the Corps, Reclamation, NRCS, and the TVA will conduct their planning) and the oversight it receives remain to be seen. For instance, it is unknown how a revised planning framework will address tradeoffs across national economic effects, environmental benefits, and public safety, as well how regional economic and social effects might be weighed. Whether the WRDA 2007 provision results in greater consideration of nonstructural measures and broadening of planning to include alternatives outside of an agency's mission, as recommended by the Commission, also remains unknown. Numerous already enacted provisions supporting nonstructural measures have produced little shift toward their full consideration and selection in water resources planning, thus indicating that authorizing provisions and statements of planning policy, without oversight and funding, may not be sufficient to produce significant change.

With some exceptions, water resource and water quality planning and implementation efforts continue to be performed separately. Although the NWC discussed preservation, it did not predict the evolution of ecosystem restoration as a significant water resources planning challenge. The growth of ecosystem restoration has precipitated a deviation from the economic basis of the 1983 Principles and Guidelines; the basic justification for restoration is not economic but environmental. For example, the Corps has developed its own guidance, which often broadly assumes that the environmental benefits exceed their economic costs, thereby negating the need for a benefit-cost analysis to justify undertaking a project based on national economic benefits. In order to evaluate and select a restoration alternative, the analysis is based on cost-effectiveness, which instead identifies which alternative provides a unit of environmental benefit at least cost. Cost-effectiveness, therefore, helps determine the efficient project design given unlimited fiscal resources, but provides little insight into whether, given constrained fiscal resources, the nation should invest in a particular restoration effort compared to other restoration opportunities. Whether implementation of WRDA 2007 provisions may assist in integrating water resources and water quality planning, and in structuring the planning and evaluation of restoration projects, is unknown.

Consistent with the recommendation by the Commission, Congress in the Water Resources Development Act of 1974 (P.L. 93-251) made the discount rate for federal water projects the one-year average yield of long-term government securities. This discount rate remains controversial. Some economists argue that the rate should reflect displacement of private investment, which is usually higher than long-term government securities. Recently, the Treasury-based rate has been lower than the rate of return on private investments or the Office of Management and Budget's base rate of 7%.[28] The benefits of moving to a different rate, which may affect the evaluation and selection of a project, and federal participation in it, continue to be debated.

Federal Water Resource Planning Activities

Following the 1965 Water Resources Planning Act (P.L. 89-80; 42 U.S.C. § 1962), the federal government supported federal, state, and river basin planning in numerous ways. By the late 1970s, federal watershed and river basin commission planning was both positively received and criticized for its costs and usefulness. Federal funding for state planning efforts began to decline. The early-1980s abandonment of the WRC and river basin commissions, as well as detailed planning standards, shifted federal project planning away from coordinated watershed-based decision making. Since then, most federal agency planning has been project-specific with some exceptions. The exceptions in the last decade include large-scale ecosystem restoration efforts at Reclamation and the Corps, and long-standing planning assistance programs like the Corps' Planning Assistance to States. Other exceptions include the NRCS small watershed program, EPA watershed activities (see "Federal Water Quality Planning Activities," below), and congressional funding of five Corps pilot watershed studies; these pilot studies are two-year, 100% federally funded, multi jurisdictional regional and watershed efforts. WRDA 1986 authorized the Corps to assess water resource needs of river basins and watersheds; this authority, however, has gone largely unused and unfunded.

In the late 1990s, the Western Water Policy Review Advisory Commission (WWPRAC) reviewed existing planning for and coordination of federal water resource projects by recommending a pilot program using a tiered or "nested" approach to water resources governance based on watersheds and river basins.[29] The WWPRAC recognized the many watershed initiatives, watershed councils, and other partnerships that had developed over the years and believed they held "much promise."[30] Along with a new governance structure based on hydrologic systems and linking basin and watershed activities, the WWPRAC recommended new coordination of basin-level federal activities, in part via appointment of a key official at the presidential or secretarial level to coordinate agency activities.[31] These suggestions were not well received by committee leaders in Congress. In a letter expressing "strong opposition to [the final WWPRAC] report," the chairmen of the Senate Appropriations Committee and House Resources Committee postulated that such recommendations would result in more bureaucracy and less state and local control.[32] Thus, the WWPRAC recommendations were not implemented; however, state and local action watershed activities and some partnerships with the federal government continue to occur.

In recent years, there has been a trend toward congressional support for technical assistance, in particular using federal agencies' engineering and design expertise to support water supply and treatment. For example, since 1992, Congress has authorized and funded the Corps to provide technical assistance for municipal water and wastewater projects in selected locations. Also in 1992, Congress created a Reclamation program to investigate opportunities for water reuse in the West, including the design and construction of demonstration and permanent facilities. These planning and related construction activities have raised questions regarding the use of federal staff and funds for design of projects that are managed separately from the agencies' typical planning framework and that support municipal and industrial water supply, which typically has been treated as a local responsibility. (See "General Water Resource User Fee and Cost-Share Policies" for a discussion of questions raised by these authorizations related to uniformity across federal agencies and project purposes.)

Some states and basins have found themselves in conflict particularly during droughts, as demands on water resources have increased. Some states, such as California, Texas, and Florida, have undertaken their own planning efforts. In recent years, these efforts have often been geared toward water supply augmentation, restoration of significant ecosystems, and drought management. Federal agency participation in state and local planning efforts, much less creating federal-state-local planning organizations as recommended by the Commission, has been constrained by the focus of the budget and appropriations process on specific projects, rather than broader planning efforts. Provisions in WRDA 2007 (e.g., Corps assistance for update of the Oklahoma state water plan) and other legislation (e.g., DOI water supply needs assessment for Alaska in P.L. 110-229, the Consolidated Natural Resources Act of 2008) illustrate ongoing examples of occasional congressional support for federal assistance with state and local planning, albeit on an ad hoc basis.

In summary, in 1973, regional and watershed planning was embedded within the executive branch water resource mission agencies, the WRC, and the federal river basin commissions and supported by a program of federal grants to develop state planning capacity. Now federal planning is primarily project-specific, with the most notable exception being large-scale ecosystem restoration efforts. Federal support for watershed and state planning is now largely ad hoc and congressionally directed.

Federal Water Quality Planning Activities

While Principles and Guidelines apply to the four federal water resource agencies (Corps, Reclamation, NRCS, and TVA), other laws address water quality and pollution control planning. (See, for example, the planning subsection under "Improvements to Water Quality.") However, because the federal government does not construct water quality projects receiving funding from EPA, there is no comparable planning and evaluation guidance to the water resource project Principles and Guidelines.

Accounting for the Environment in Project Development[33]

Issue

The Commission, in Chapter 6 of its final report, discusses issues associated with the need to balance water resources project development and environmental values.[34] The Commission found that project development needs tended to dominate over concerns about the potential environmental impacts of a project (see also "Water and the Natural Environment," below). A mechanism identified to help achieve a balance was the integration of the environmental review requirements of the National Environmental Policy Act (NEPA; 42 U.S.C. §§ 4321-4347) with the project development process. Although the Commission recognized NEPA as a potential tool to include environmental concerns in the decision-making process, it also identified how certain elements of the NEPA process could contribute delays, uncertainty, and challenges to project development. For example, it identified challenges associated with appropriately determining all "reasonable" project alternatives. To understand the Commission's recommendations on this issue it is important to understand some of NEPA's requirements, particularly as they were understood and being implemented in 1973. A brief explanation of these requirements is found in the **Appendix** of this report. (See also, CRS Report RL33152, *The National Environmental Policy Act (NEPA): Background and Implementation*, by Linda Luther and CRS Report RL33267, *The National Environmental Policy Act: Streamlining NEPA*, by Linda Luther.)

NWC Recommendations

The Commission recommendations reflect the NEPA compliance difficulties that many agencies were facing in the early 1970s. The NWC identified processes intended to clarify NEPA requirements and expedite the environmental review process for water projects. Generally, the recommendations specify:[35]

- how elements of the NEPA process should be integrated into the licensing process;
- certain measures regarding public and congressional participation; and
- the need for hearings on challenges associated with determining the appropriate range of reasonable projects.

Current Status and Implementation

Many of these recommendations were subsequently addressed, particularly through NEPA-related case law and promulgation of regulations to implement NEPA's EIS requirements in 1978. Specifically, since the Commission report was issued, a host of court decisions, the promulgation of Council of Environmental Quality's (CEQ's) NEPA regulations, and the implementation of NEPA regulations by individual agencies have contributed to the development of a now-mature NEPA process for water resources projects. Elements of that process address many of the recommendations made by the Commission. For example, CEQ's regulations were intended to foster better decision-making and reduce the paperwork and delays associated with NEPA compliance.[36] Also, among other requirements, NEPA regulations:

- defined and specified the roles of "lead agencies" (those responsible for preparing the NEPA documentation) and "cooperating agencies" (agencies that participate in or contribute to the preparation of the NEPA documentation);
- allowed lead agencies to set time limits on milestones in the NEPA process and page limits on documentation;
- specified environmental review procedures and documents applicable to projects that had uncertain or insignificant environmental impacts;
- specified how an agency was to involve the public in the NEPA process (e.g., specified at what points public input should be solicited and accepted); and
- specified criteria that must be addressed when providing an analysis of project alternatives.

Also, the CEQ regulations specified the required elements of an EIS, which include:

- a brief statement, developed by the lead agency, specifying the underlying purpose of a project and the need to which the agency is responding;
- a discussion of the range of alternatives, including the proposed action, that will meet the project's purpose and need—a discussion that should explore and objectively evaluate all "reasonable" alternatives;
- a succinct description of the environment of the area(s) to be affected by the alternatives under consideration; and
- an analysis of impacts of each alternative on the affected environment, including a discussion of the probable beneficial and adverse social, economic, and environmental effects of each alternative.

The degree to which the CEQ regulations have expedited the NEPA process is still debated. Since 1973, NEPA's procedural requirements may have become clearer, but the overall process is more complicated for reasons that have little to do with NEPA itself. For example, water resources projects are likely to be large, complex projects that may involve compliance with a host of other environmental requirements (many promulgated after June 1973). To integrate the compliance process and avoid duplication of effort, NEPA regulations specify that, to the fullest extent possible, agencies must prepare the EIS concurrently with *any* environmental requirements.[37] The EIS must list any federal permits, licenses, and other government certification required to implement the proposed project. In this capacity NEPA functions as an "umbrella" statute, meaning that any study, review, or consultation required by any other environmental law should be conducted within the framework of the NEPA process.

NEPA's overarching nature often leads to confusion as to how it relates to other laws. As an umbrella statute, NEPA forms the framework to coordinate or demonstrate compliance with other environmental requirements. NEPA itself does not *require* compliance with them. If, theoretically, the requirement to comply with NEPA were removed, compliance with each applicable law would remain. For example, a required element of the EIS is to determine whether biological consultation is required under ESA. The requirement to comply with ESA would simply be *identified* by the NEPA process; the obligation to comply with the law remains under the ESA.

Some environmental review issues identified by the Commission remain at issue. For example, for individual projects, agencies may still have challenges in sufficiently identifying all "reasonable" project alternatives.

Although there are more specific criteria to make that determination, it is something that must be determined on a project-by-project basis. It may form the basis of litigation if project stakeholders feel that an alternative they would prefer is not considered but, to them, is reasonable. Also, the threat of litigation is sometimes an issue in EIS preparation. Agencies may prepare NEPA documentation that is overly inclusive and lengthy in an attempt to avoid litigation challenging the sufficiency of the analyses or review of alternatives.

Public Participation in Water Resources Planning[38]

Issue
    The Commission, in a section of Chapter 10, addressed concerns regarding public participation in water resources planning. It discussed deficiencies in public participation and acknowledged certain limits and requirements to avoid delays in project implementation.

NWC Recommendations
    The NWC sought to clarify public participation requirements as well as set parameters to avoid excessive delay. The Commission made a number of recommendations:

- Federal water resources agencies should adopt procedures and issue appropriate directives to field entities to provide opportunities for broad public participation in water planning activities "from the inception of the planning process on."
- As a prerequisite to project authorization, Congress should require agencies to report on public participation with respect to particular projects, showing compliance with agency public participation procedures, describing the questions considered and the viewpoints expressed, and providing supporting information for the decisions reached on controversial points.
- Water resources planning agencies should structure their planning procedures to promptly resolve and conclude issues by timing the public participation and defining issues to be addressed.
- Water resources planning agencies should help compensate for the lack of financial, technical, and manpower resources of participants

by providing timely, well-publicized information, scheduling at least
one public hearing near the proposed project, and making basic data
readily available.

- Federal and state governments should require advance public
  disclosure on the pre-license planning of major nonfederal projects
  expected to have an impact on water resources.
- Licensing agencies should seek to develop the interests of all
  participants affected by agencies' decisions.

Current Status and Implementation

Many of the public participation concerns raised by the Commission have
been addressed through the current NEPA process. For example, as the law
has been interpreted, one of NEPA's primary goals is to allow the public a
meaningful opportunity to learn about and comment on the proposed federal
actions *before* decisions are made and actions taken (e.g., during the project
planning and evaluation process). To meet this goal, CEQ's regulations require
agencies to encourage and facilitate public involvement in decisions that
significantly affect the quality of the human environment (i.e., projects that
require an EIS).[39] Specifically, agencies are required to provide public notice
of NEPA-related hearings, public meetings, and the availability of
environmental documents.[40] Documentation of public participation must be
included in the final EIS. Although the Corps and other agencies had some
processes requiring public review prior to NEPA, NEPA greatly expanded the
public review and input process. CEQ has guidance educating the public on its
rights with regard to participation.[41]

Generally, public participation opportunities are available during the
initial project scoping process and after a draft EIS has been produced (not
throughout the entire project planning and development process). If
stakeholders have concerns about a proposed plan's impacts, their comments
may be directed at virtually any element of that plan, the NEPA process, or
related documentation. If stakeholders believe their concerns have been
inadequately addressed, they may sue. To avoid conflict after a project has
reached an advanced stage of planning, CEQ recommends that continuous
contact with non-agency stakeholders be maintained from the earliest planning
stages up to the decision to select a particular alternative.

CEQ regulations specify public involvement requirements only for federal
actions requiring an EIS. Agencies may devise their own public involvement
policies for environmental assessments (which are an allowable alternative to
an EIS under certain circumstances) or in making a categorical exclusion

determination. If a project does not require an EIS but still has garnered public attention, agencies generally involve the public in ways similar to its EIS methods.

Federal Water Resources Coordination[42]

Issue

The Commission recommended federal organizational changes to improve efficiency and to meet future challenges for the planning, development, and management of the nation's water and related land resources. The Commission found the then-active WRC an important and useful mechanism; however, it recommended changes to help the WRC better fulfill its roles of coordinating and appraising water policies and programs and of planning the conservation and development of the nation's water resources. The Commission cited and agreed with numerous previous studies in supporting the independent review of federal water development proposals. The Commission found three areas in which the functions of federal agencies needed modifying.

NWC Recommendations

The Commission recommended for the WRC's structure:

- creation of an independent, full-time chairman on the staff of the White House reporting directly to the President;
- placement in the Executive Office of the President; and
- expansion of statutory membership to add the Secretaries and Administrators of Commerce, Housing and Urban Development, EPA, and Atomic Energy Commission, and eliminate the membership of the Secretary of Health.

The Commission recommended the following actions to facilitate the WRC's task:

- authority to distribute planning funds;
- extension of the authorization and removal of the appropriations cap on its grant program to support state water planning;
- submission of a consolidated grant application for each state seeking funds from federal agencies for water planning and programs;

- authority for the WRC chairman to coordinate federal participation in the river basin and water management compacts; and
- authority for the WRC chairman to chair an independent review board examining federal water development proposals, river basin plans, and grant programs and make recommendations on their need, feasibility, and utility to the President and Congress.

The Commission recommended eliminating duplication in the collection and distribution of basic water data; better managing the similar engineering functions in federal water resources agencies, and concentrating dispersed water technology efforts. Specifically, it recommended:

- combining NOAA and USGS into a new DOI agency responsible for water resources data, moving NOAA's fisheries functions to the FWS, and having NOAA's coastal zone management functions be part of the land planning functions of the federal government;
- shifting USDA water engineering functions (e.g., reservoir design, channelization) to nonfederal entities;
- shifting Reclamation from a construction agency toward an agency operating federal facilities efficiently in water-short regions;
- limiting the Corps to only design and construction that cannot be efficiently performed by nonfederal entities and increase its nonstructural and nonfederal assistance actions; and
- creating an Office of Water Technology by combining existing water research offices and activities placed in the DOI with a charter broad enough to meet other federal research needs.

Current Status and Implementation
Since 1973, significant shifts have occurred in the federal water resources institutional arrangements and organizations; however, the federalist division of responsibilities has remained largely intact. As recommended by the Commission, the WRC was located in the Executive Office of the President and membership was expanded in 1975 to include the Secretaries of Commerce, Housing and Urban Development, and Transportation, and the EPA Administrator. The WRC has not been funded or active since 1983; however, the authorization for the WRC still exists.

By 1973, implementation of the Water Resources Planning Act of 1965 (P.L. 89-80; 42 U.S.C. § 1962) had increased the coordination and planning of federal actions, particularly through the creation of the WRC. The 1965 act created the WRC and numerous river basin commissions charged with watershed planning. There has been no legislation comprehensively changing federal water resources since that act. Instead, the shifts in organizations and institutional arrangements came about from executive branch actions and incremental changes through legislation. Their cumulative effect has been a decrease since the 1970s of coordination of federal water agency activities and planning.

Following years of decreasing support for river basin commission efforts, President Reagan in Executive Order 12319 ordered the termination in 1981 of six of the commissions created by the 1965 act and the transition of their activities to the member states. This effectively eliminated the federal river basin and broad-based watershed planning efforts.[43] During this time, federal grants for state planning activities also largely disappeared. Since these changes, federal agency participation in planning and negotiation efforts within watersheds and between states has been constrained by the focus on specific projects. What remains of the federal planning assistance generally is a few programs scattered among several agencies. (See "Water Resources Project Planning and Evaluation," above, for additional analysis.)

Review of federal water projects also has experienced many shifts since 1973. There is no entity that independently reviews water projects by all federal agencies. The Corps has maintained its construction program, although not at its 1960s level, and may continue to have significant construction responsibilities as it improves aging infrastructure, retools earlier projects to balance environmental needs, and is called on to provide flood and hurricane storm risk reduction projects. However, changes in the late 1980s and early 1990s reduced the level of review of Corps projects. For example, Congress eliminated the Corps-staffed Board of Engineers for Rivers and Harbors, which had reviewed the civil works plans from 1902 until WRDA 1992. Review continued to occur under the 1981 E.O. 12322, which requires that a Corps feasibility report be reviewed by the Office of Management and Budget (OMB) for consistency with the policies and programs of the President, planning guidelines, laws, and regulations. Following criticisms of a number of Corps planning studies for faulty analysis and New Orleans floodwall failures in 2005, Congress created in WRDA 2007 a process for external independent review of many Corps planning studies and for ongoing safety reviews during construction of significant flood and storm damage projects. How these provisions are implemented is still being determined. The WRDA 2007 reviews are limited to technical analysis and do not include a policy review.

As the Commission predicted, Reclamation too has moved more toward management and has a less substantial construction function than it did in the 1950s and 1960s. In 1987, Reclamation formally adopted a new mission statement recognizing its increased role in water resources management vis-à-vis construction. Recent Reclamation efforts have included working with other DOI, federal agencies, and nonfederal parties, including Tribes, to resolve water conflicts through settlement agreements and assisting with water supply augmentation technologies (e.g., Reclamation's water reuse program and its desalination research program).

The NWC recommendations that NOAA's responsibilities be divided among other agencies were not implemented. The challenge of accomplishing organizational changes like the Commission's NOAA recommendations was seen when the Secretary of the Interior in the mid-1990s attempted to consolidate the biological research being conducted by DOI's various agencies into a single agency. The effort was met with much resistance and skepticism, eventually being scaled back to creating a new biological division within the U.S. Geological Survey. While the channelization program at the USDA largely disappeared, USDA watershed efforts have continued. Specifically, USDA's NRCS cooperates with states and local agencies to carry out engineering works to improve flood control and water use, including dam rehabilitation. Dam repair and safety remain areas of growing engineering and construction not only for NRCS but also for Reclamation and the Corps.

The Commission's recommendation to limit Corps design and construction activities to those that cannot be efficiently performed by nonfederal entities generally has not been a criterion used during authorization and appropriations. For example, Congress has authorized and appropriated funds for Corps participation in design and construction of municipal drinking water and wastewater projects. In the United States, drinking water and wastewater systems generally are the responsibility of municipalities; their design and construction are performed by the municipalities or their private engineering consultants (albeit sometimes with federal financial support). In an effort to define the scope of the Corps' involvement in the growing area of ecosystem restoration, the G. W. Bush Administration in recent budgets used as one of its criteria for restoration projects that the Corps be uniquely well suited to perform the work.

The Commission's recommendation to increase the Corps' nonfederal assistance actions has not been implemented. The Corps has retained its Planning Assistance to States program and its Flood Plain Management Service, which in recent years have averaged roughly $6 million each in annual appropriations. However, this funding level represents a decline in federal support for these activities. In the mid-1970s, the Corps received roughly $30 million (in 2007 dollars) for regional planning and planning assistance to states, with another $30 million (in 2007 dollars) for its Flood Plain Management Service.

In 1974, the Office of Water Research and Technology was formed in DOI through consolidation of some of the offices identified by the Commission. The Office of Water Research and Technology was abolished in 1982 and the desalination research program transferred to Reclamation. Since the 1960s and 1970s, the topical balance of the federal water research has shifted from social science topics (e.g., water demand, water institutions) and water supply augmentation and conservation (e.g., desalination), to water quality.[44] Also since the early 1970s, the amount of the federal budget dedicated to all types of water research has been halved.[45]

Aspects of water resources have remained scattered across congressional committees, in a pattern generally similar to the fragmented arrangement in 1973, which the Commission did not find particularly problematic.[46] Since 1973, other institutional and organization changes that are not specific to water resources, yet affect water resources, have occurred. For example, executive branch oversight and management direction in the water resources field has evolved. In particular, the Office of Management and Budget in 1973 functioned as an agency with dual management and budget missions. A reorganization in the 1990s reduced the distinction between management staff and budgetary staff; this resulted in less management oversight and in the administrations' budget policy influencing both the short and long-term guidance provided to water resources agencies.

Without the WRC, CEQ at times and other ad hoc mechanisms have been used to arbitrate and coordinate among federal agencies on water issues; however, there is no institutionally recognized system for conducting such coordination. The organizational landscape of water management also has shifted as a result of increased consideration of environmental issues; the Environmental Protection Agency (EPA), created in 1970, has the lead federal role in protecting the quality of the nation's environment. In selected cases, EPA has influenced the implementation of federal water resources projects. EPA has also become a significant force in shaping a wide range of state, local, and private project planning and design through the agency's implementation of its water quality and wetlands permitting responsibilities.

Water Resources Authorizations, Budget, and Appropriations[47]

Issue

The Commission found that the steps by which separate branches of government conceived and executed water resources projects needed to be closely linked, or coordinated, to efficiently use the nation's water and fiscal resources. According to the Commission, the budgeting procedures neither reflected nor promoted regional or long-term water resources development. The Commission instead found that projects often were presented and considered individually. The Commission concluded that an annual appropriations process unnecessarily subjected construction completion to uncertainty as well as to both cost and lengthening of schedules ("schedule growth"). It found that a backlog of projects planned and evaluated under obsolete guidance and criteria overburdened the appropriations process and allowed initiation of projects that no longer merited the required investment. The Commission concluded that congressional politics and behavior tended toward particularized and fragmented decision-making.

NWC Recommendations

The Commission recommended:

- using comprehensive river basin and regional development plans as the basis for authorization and appropriations for both individual projects and broader programs;
- incorporating into budgeting the 20 major regions used by the WRC for planning;
- moving from an annual construction appropriations process to full-cost budgeting;
- giving federal program administrators authority to contract in advance of appropriations for programs meeting national objectives;
- requiring five-year agency programs for existing and new construction projects;
- requiring a five-year national budget for the multi-agency federal water program;
- deauthorizing construction not begun within 10 years of authorization; and
- reevaluating plans authorized more than five years before construction.

Current Status and Implementation

Although some of the Commission's recommendations have been attempted, the basic functioning of the authorization, budgeting, and appropriations processes for water resources has not changed significantly since 1973. The consideration of project authorizations and appropriations as part of comprehensive river basin and regional development plans has not been practiced since the early 1980s, when most of those larger-scale federal water resources planning efforts were halted. (See "Water Resources Project Planning and Evaluation" for more information.) Project authorizations and appropriations generally still are considered on a project-specific basis. For example, although there is regular congressional consideration of an omnibus WRDA, the legislation consists mostly of authorizations of individual Corps study and construction projects. While there have been provisions in WRDAs that address policy issues, the authorizations generally are not considered as part of a comprehensive plan or review of Corps or federal water resources activities. The same is true for occasional omnibus Reclamation legislation.

Budgeting for water resource projects also has remained project-specific, with some exceptions for large-scale restoration efforts such as some Everglades restoration funding. For example, Reclamation budgets consist of projects grouped by regions, but budgeting is not founded on regional resource plans. In recent years, the G. W. Bush Administration proposed funding the Corps operations and maintenance account based on hydrologic regions; however, this approach has not been adopted in enacted appropriations, due largely to concerns about a lack of transparency in how the regional requests were developed and about transparency in how regional appropriations would be implemented.

Full-cost budgets and appropriations for water resources projects generally have not been used. A significant exception is the full funding via supplemental appropriations of the repair and strengthening of coastal storm protection facilities in New Orleans after Hurricane Katrina.

Congress has used general contract authority to varying degrees for different programs. For many water programs since 1973, Congress has tightened its controls of contract authority in an attempt to preserve the congressional role in guiding appropriations. For instance, Congress recently has enacted more stringent rules for Corps multi-year contracts.

Water resource agencies, along with many other agencies, have produced five-year strategic plans in response to the Government Performance and Results Act of 1994 (P.L. 103-62). These plans are not capital budgeting plans, instead they focus on agency mission, goals, and performance. There have

been few efforts at capital budgeting by water resource agencies, and no
sustained effort for coordinated budgeting for the entire federal water program.

Congress has passed legislation requiring deauthorization of Corps
construction projects that have not received appropriations for six years.
Without other changes being enacted and with the continuation of
authorization of individual projects, this deauthorization process has neither
quelled the construction backlog nor ensured that construction activities satisfy
current planning requirements. Reclamation has no general deauthorization
process for unfunded projects; however, in limited cases, Reclamation
authorizations contain a "sunset" provision.

Because the G. W. Bush Administration had a "no new start" policy in
recent Corps budgets, the vast majority of new construction projects have been
initiated by congressional appropriations. There has been no requirement that
new construction starts that were authorized many years prior be re-evaluated.

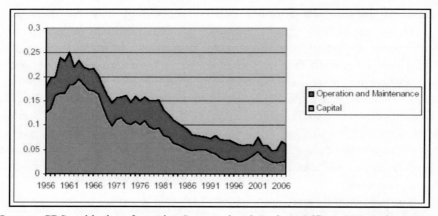

Source: CRS, with data from the Congressional Budget Office, CBO Infrastructure
    Spending   Supplemental   Tables,   2008   Update,   available   at
    http://www.cbo.gov/doc.cfm?index=9135.

Figure 2. Federal Water Resources Spending as a Percentage of GDP (1956 -2007)

The backlog of construction authorizations created tension between the G.
W. Bush Administration, whose Corps budget concentrated funding on a
smaller set of projects, and Congress, which applied a more distributed
approach by appropriating to a larger set of projects and activities. An
argument for concentrated appropriations is that the lower funding levels that
individual projects receive under the distributed approach delay construction

progress, resulting in increased cost and schedule growth, which represent lost economic efficiency. Those supporting a more distributed appropriations process, however, assert that a geographical and jurisdictional dispersal of projects maintains the currency and relevance of the Corps' mission. Furthermore, tradeoffs in economic efficiency, equity, and political feasibility have implicitly occurred to some degree during the development of the Corps' annual construction appropriations. Data on cost and schedule growth of Corps civil works projects may help clarify the tradeoffs between the two approaches and identify improved opportunities for project management; however, little aggregated or systematic data about cost or schedule growth is available.

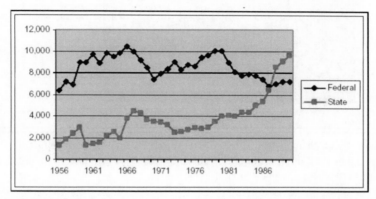

Source: CRS, with data from the Congressional Budget Office, CBO Infrastructure Spending Supplemental Tables, 2008 Update, available at http://www.cbo.gov/doc.cfm?index=9135.

Figure 3. Federal and State (and Local) Spending on Water Resources, 1956-1990 (in millions of 2006 dollars)

Annual federal appropriations (not including supplemental appropriations) for water resources projects followed a declining trend after the mid-1960s, as a percentage of both gross domestic product (GDP) (**Figure 2**) and discretionary spending. During the 1970s and 1980s, nonfederal spending increased (**Figure 3**) in response to numerous forces including new federal standards for water quality and related municipal water and wastewater infrastructure investments. Environmental litigation and resource constraints have focused much of the new authorization and appropriation for water resources efforts on resolving multi-use resource conflicts and addressing new and instream demands. Safety and rehabilitation of aging federal infrastructure is a growing part of the agencies' budgets and appropriations. Aging local infrastructure and interest in nonfederal dam removal are currently addressed, often on an ad hoc basis, by Congress through individual authorizations and annual appropriations for water resources agencies. The shift in federal water resources spending from construction to maintenance is evident in **Figure 4**.

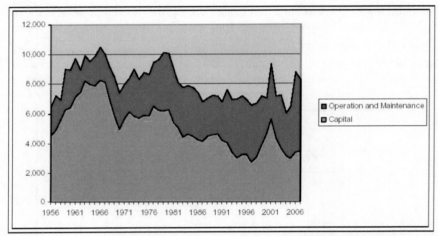

Source: CRS, with data from the Congressional Budget Office, CBO Infrastructure Spending Supplemental Tables, 2008 Update, available at http://www.cbo.gov/doc.cfm?index=9135.

Figure 4. Federal Water Resources Construction and Maintenance Spending (1956-2007, in millions of 2006 dollars)

WATER AND THE NATURAL ENVIRONMENT

The Commission's report (primarily in Chapter 2) addressed the environmental impacts of water projects and water resource agency activities. The Commission noted negative impacts (e.g., alteration of stream habitat) as well as positive ones (e.g., recreational benefits of a reservoir). It found that the federal government insufficiently addressed ecological processes and environmental values in its water project and permitting decisions. Yet the Commission also noted that economic values and public safety often were at stake when choosing among water resource alternatives. The Commission identified three areas for improvement:

- understanding and predicting the primary environmental impacts of water programs, uses, projects, and their alternatives;
- assessing the secondary and broader environmental effects of these actions; and
- incorporating environmental values and processes into decision-making.

The report specifically discussed the environmental effects of reservoir development, flood policy, water development in estuarine and coastal ecosystems, water project effects on fish and wildlife, and channelization.[48] A related topic is the Commission's recommendations for addressing fish and wildlife values in project planning. The Commission's overarching concern that environmental impacts be analyzed in the decision-making process also is addressed in "Accounting for the Environment in Project Development," above, which discusses implementation of NEPA.

Since 1973, water resources development has slowed, and federal appropriations shifted from development to environmental preservation and operation and maintenance of infrastructure. Many of the concerns raised by the NWC have been addressed via implementation of environmental laws. Many large federal water actions are for ecosystem restoration and stream rehabilitation. Whether these changes and efforts have adequately addressed the Commission's concerns is a matter of disagreement. The degree to which development and environmental protection tradeoffs are evaluated and weighed remains central to many current water resources conflicts.

Reservoir Development[49]

Issue

Chapter 2 of the Commission report includes a section on reservoir development. Creating a reservoir, by impounding water behind a dam or diverting it to an off-stream storage site, generally alters a river's aquatic and riparian ecosystems, sometimes benefitting some species and ecosystems while harming others. Reservoirs inundate habitat and alter ecosystem properties by changing flow regimes, water temperature, and water quality. Changes in ecosystems due to reservoir construction can result in biodiversity loss and changes in species composition.

Downstream of reservoirs, altered flows can change native fisheries and habitat. Dams creating reservoirs also can prevent the migration of fish species up-or downstream. The Commission also noted the social effects of reservoir development; reservoirs change the types of recreation opportunities available and the aesthetics of the landscape. The Commission believed that these alterations or effects should be considered when contemplating water resource decisions.

NWC Recommendations
The Commission's recommendations for reservoir development were to:

- develop a comprehensive database of the condition of the nation's waters that encompasses water quality and quantity, ecological processes, and environmental attributes;
- further research environmental impacts of water resource development;
- adopt planning techniques that account for ecological processes and environmental values;
- analyze environmental impacts of proposed projects and their alternatives;
- promote decision-making in the face of uncertainty; and
- monitor environmental consequences of projects post-construction.

Current Status and Implementation
Neither a national-level data set documenting the extent to which waterways have been channelized and impounded (and the effects of these measures) nor a national database of ecological and environmental conditions of waterways has been implemented.[50] Although there is not a national database, understanding of how reservoirs and their operations affect fisheries and habitat is much improved, and significantly more information on the state of the nation's waters is available today than in 1973.

The Commission's recommendations regarding accounting for ecological values and analyzing environmental impacts today are considered largely through implementation of NEPA and ESA during project planning and evaluations necessary for major changes in project operations. Both NEPA and the ESA require extensive assessment of project impacts on the environment and consideration of alternative actions; however, there is no requirement to protect the overall function of such ecosystems and some argue that full accounting of ecosystem effects in project planning could still be improved. Few new large-scale U.S. reservoirs are currently under construction, although some are being considered, particularly in the West. Consequently, reservoir planning in recent decades has largely focused on balancing competing objectives in operation and management of existing reservoirs (as opposed to planning new projects), and in some cases managing for new objectives. For example, actions required to protect threatened or endangered species listed under the ESA have been significant drivers for many changes in operating plans. Conflicting objectives of operating Missouri River locks and dams—namely, maintaining flows for navigation and restricting or otherwise changing flows to protect seasonal needs of some bird species—required controversial updates to the Missouri River reservoir control manual to provide for barge traffic and other purposes. Similar operational changes are occurring with salmon runs in the Sacramento and Columbia River basins and fishes in the California Bay-Delta, sometimes pitting one species against another.

Data

The Commission called for collecting and organizing a broad range of data on the condition of the nation's water. The Commission report suggested including not only water quantity and quality factors but also geological attributes, soil properties, riparian vegetation, fisheries and climate factors, aesthetics, related land uses, and recreation use. Although a national database was never developed, broad data sets have been developed in some regions with high data demands due to resource conflicts. For example, some federal restoration initiatives, such as in the Florida Everglades and the Bay-Delta in California, have resulted in the documentation and monitoring of a wide range of ecosystem and environmental conditions. Nonetheless, according to many experts, improvements in understanding, modeling, and predicting the interaction of water project operations and ecosystem health continue to be needed and pursued.[51]

Some basic water flow data are being collected on a national level. As in 1973, water flows in streams and rivers continue to be measured by a network of roughly 7,500 stream gages and are reported through the National Streamflow Information Program administered by the U.S. Geological Survey (USGS). Many of the gages use collection and communication technologies that have significantly improved since 1973. For example, most report real-time stream flows, thus improving their usefulness for forecasting river conditions, issuing flood warnings, and planning reservoir releases or water withdrawals. However, the streamflow program is based on partnerships with local sponsors and is not comprehensive. Additionally, the program is often a target of budget-cutting efforts. While Congress typically restores funding in annual appropriations, overall levels of federal funding and the number of stream gages have declined in recent years.

The USGS also works with states to estimate water withdrawals and assess water quality[52] in various water bodies. Data on trends in freshwater fisheries are available, but generally are reported on a species-specific basis rather than by watershed or ecosystem, unless they are part of a specific plan. Data are also collected on wetland losses due to human activities such as agriculture, urban development, and water resources projects.[53]

Attempts have been made to better coordinate data collection and improve the quality of information collected. For example, OMB Circular No. 92-01 established a national "Advisory Committee on Water Information" to coordinate and improve data collection. The committee is made up of federal agency representatives, state interests, academics, and industry professional organizations. The committee meets regularly to advise federal government officials on federal water information programs.[54]

Environmental Values in Planning and Decision-Making

The Commission recommended analyzing the environmental impacts of water resources proposals and their alternatives as part of its 1973 final report. This recommendation was not new. NEPA, which became law in early 1970, required documentation of the environmental impacts of federal actions, but its implementation remained in its infancy at the time of the NWC report. Since then, NEPA implementation has resulted in a more comprehensive environmental analysis of project plans, similar to what the NWC and others had recommended. Implementation of the ESA has also been a significant driver in incorporating species and some habitat issues into the analysis of reservoir plans and operations. Taken together, these laws have fundamentally changed the way in which project impacts are evaluated. Non-federal interests play a much larger role than previously, and in some cases have become active "partners" in the decision-making process.

Even so, water resource planning continues to be criticized for a narrow focus on national economic development benefits or specific development objectives and insufficient evaluation and weighing of environmental and social concerns (such as public safety and social equity). The 110th Congress, in the Water Resources Development Act of 2007 (WRDA 2007, P.L. 110-114), called for the Secretary of the Army to update water resources planning principles and guidelines to better account for the environment and for projects to be justified based only on public benefits. The updated planning principles and guidelines would apply only to those planning studies begun after issuance and only to Corps projects. There remains no review process for previously authorized projects or projects undertaken by other federal water resource agencies. (See also "Water Resources Project Planning and Evaluation" and "Accounting for the Environment in Project Development.")

In general, reservoir planning efforts and other water resources planning have responded to environmental concerns by trying to minimize and mitigate harm, rather than avoiding harm and improving existing environmental conditions. A major exception has been the planning of ecosystem restoration projects. Even so, many of the largest ecosystem restoration projects are at least in part aimed at restoring habitat and other conditions degraded by past water resource development projects. How to evaluate the costs and benefits of ecosystem projects remains a challenge; a current debate is whether and how to value losses and gains in ecosystem services[55] during water resource project evaluation and decision-making.

The Commission contended that research will not always result in a definitive understanding of the environmental impacts of water projects. It recommended that planners reach a decision on a project based on the best available science, even if uncertainties exist. Tension remains over when there is sufficient research, monitoring, and modeling to make decisions on whether and how to proceed with a project or operational change.

Some recent planning efforts have used adaptive management as a tool to address decision-making in the face of environmental uncertainty. Adaptive management is the process of incorporating new scientific and programmatic information into the implementation of a plan. It is a management approach that allows flexibility to adjust strategies during implementation if goals are not being met or if new circumstances arise. The flexibility inherent in adaptive management, however, remains controversial. Concerns with using adaptive management include the potential for cost growth of restoration efforts, the delegation of decisions to agency staff or even nonfederal parties, the water supply or water flow uncertainty for other water users, and the level of investment risk if the restoration effort fails. The use of adaptive management in water resources to date has largely been limited to select restoration efforts and has yet to be used across all types of projects and their operations.

Monitoring

The Commission stated that a project's environmental effects should be monitored post-construction. In general, federal agencies typically do not analyze the cumulative effects of a project's impacts or multiple dams on a river system until directed to do so or possibly when a significant operational change is being considered. There are some examples of trying to address ecosystem and species health through monitoring and actions prior to such a review and any required mitigation—actions to reduce or reverse damage—that might result. However, monitoring river systems and tracking effects on species raise challenging issues for rivers in which reservoirs and other development were begun prior to the enactment of most environmental laws. Such monitoring is also costly. Adaptive management techniques have been used in some cases where operational changes are necessary. In such cases, monitoring and ongoing assessment are key components used to inform decision makers. Yet, because it is often difficult to predict how much projects will cost and when they might be completed under adaptive management approaches, the use of adaptive management is particularly difficult for legislative decision makers who are accountable to the public and must justify agency expenditures and actions.

While a national program specifically targeted at monitoring the environmental impacts of water projects does not exist, WRDA 2007 includes numerous provisions that augment monitoring for newly authorized Corps of Engineers (Corps) projects. For example, WRDA 2007 required that each project have a plan for monitoring implementation and ecological success of mitigation. It also required that Corps ecosystem restoration project plans include a plan for monitoring the success of restoration efforts for 10 years after project completion, with the costs shared by the federal government and the nonfederal project sponsor. WRDA 2007 also added monitoring as an authorized activity for many specific Corps projects, including some dredged material disposal projects and coastal sediment management efforts. The impact of these provisions remains unknown, due to the early stage of their implementation.

Flood Policy[56]

The Corps and the Federal Emergency Management Agency (FEMA) are the principal federal agencies involved in programs to reduce riverine and coastal flood damages and risk. Other federal agencies, such as the U.S. Department of Agriculture's Natural Resources Conservation Service (NRCS), the Department of the Interior's Bureau of Reclamation (Reclamation), and the Tennessee Valley Authority (TVA), also are involved with flood damage reduction projects.

In the United States, flood-related roles and responsibilities are shared; local governments are responsible for land use and zoning decisions that shape floodplain and coastal development, but state and federal governments also influence community and individual decisions on managing flood risk. For example, the federal government constructs some of the nation's flood control infrastructure, supports hazard mitigation, offers flood insurance, and provides emergency response and disaster aid for significant floods. However, state and local governments largely are responsible for making land use decisions (e.g., zoning decisions) that allow or prohibit development in flood prone areas. In addition to constructing flood damage reduction infrastructure, state and local entities operate and maintain most of the flood control infrastructure and have initial flood-fighting responsibilities.

Issue

The Commission found that despite significant investments to reduce flood damages, annual flood losses grew and people continued living in harm's way. The Commission called for a fundamental reorientation in national flood policy, and for Congress, relevant agencies, and the public to commit to the broad goal of putting floodplain lands to their best use rather than allowing unfettered flood-prone development.

NWC Recommendations

The Commission recommended federal efforts that:

- encourage floodplain management that maximizes national economic, social, and environmental welfare;
- reform federal programs for flood damage reduction;[57]
- improve state floodplain management capabilities;
- encourage public, typically nonfederal, acquisition of floodplain lands for which the best use is recreation or open space;
- restrict federal construction assistance in floodplains or for flood-damaged structures until steps have been taken to avoid future damages;
- require federal programs and actions comply with floodplain plans;
- improve flood forecasting and community emergency response action plans;
- require the (then-active) WRC to develop a unified national program for basic flood data and flood damages;

- encourage coordinated land-use and floodplain planning; and
- independently appraise the National Flood Insurance Program (NFIP, P.L. 90-448, 42 U.S.C §4001 et seq.).

Current Status and Implementation

Federal efforts since 1973 have not been guided by a clearly defined flood policy or floodplain vision, as recommended by the Commission. However, many incremental changes to improve flood policy consistent with the Commission's recommendations have been enacted or adopted at all levels of government. Nonetheless, the nation's riverine and coastal flood vulnerability has increased. Incremental policy and program improvements were overwhelmed by incentives to develop floodplains and coastal areas and population and other demographic trends, or were never fully implemented or enforced. Other federal actions produced some indirect flood risk reduction benefits; for example, Congress has supported conservation efforts on agricultural lands and wetlands protection that may reduce flood damages by slowing down or temporarily storing flood waters. Whether these benefits are overwhelmed by changes in flood-prone land use (e.g., conversion of agricultural land behind levees to residential or commercial development) remains largely unknown because regional-scale and multi-agency plans and evaluations have been rare.

The fundamental reorientation for floodplain management called for by the Commission has not occurred. The institutional arrangements that in 1973 provided avenues for more coordinated federal efforts have diminished (see box, "Brief History of the Water Resources Council"). The WRC was disbanded in 1983; the Federal Interagency Task Force on Floodplain Management, which had continued some of the WRC's flood-related functions after 1983, stopped convening in the late 1990s. Federal support and opportunities for local capacity building decreased with the loss of these institutions.

However, WRDA 2007 may be an early step in a reorientation of flood policy if its provisions are implemented. The legislation calls for a report describing flood risk and comparing regional risks. The report also is to assess the effectiveness of flood efforts and programs, analyze whether programs encourage development in flood-prone areas, and provide recommendations. The challenge may be less to develop the report's content and more to achieve action on its findings and recommendations. Numerous reports have recommended reducing flood vulnerability, especially following the devastating 1993 Midwest floods and significant hurricanes.[58] Generally, these reports' narrower recommendations, rather than their broader calls for change, are the only ones implemented.

Since 1973, numerous legislative provisions and administrative actions have addressed flood risk. These actions include supporting nonstructural flood damage reduction, augmenting hazard mitigation activities, fostering floodplain regulation, and guiding federal actions in floodplains (e.g., E.O. 11988). Many of these, however, have seen only marginal implementation, enforcement, and funding. This marginal action to reduce risk has been overwhelmed by the growth of the number of lives, property, and infrastructure in flood-prone areas; significant outlays for disaster relief; and increased potential for social and economic disruption from hurricanes and floods. (For more information, see CRS Report RL33129, *Flood Risk Management and Levees: A Federal Primer*, by Betsy A. Cody and Nicole T. Carter.)

Generally, congressional oversight, administrative implementation, and federal appropriations have reflected a reactive and fragmented approach to flooding. Flood policy continues to be dominated by structural flood damage reduction investments (e.g., levee building), the NFIP, and federal disaster aid, rather than a comprehensive flood risk and floodplain management approach (e.g., restricting unnecessary development in floodplains). Current arrangements of aid, insurance, and water resources projects are criticized for providing disincentives to "wise use" of flood-prone areas.[59] This is in contrast to the Commission's support for a focused and coordinated effort to reduce the cost of flooding on the economy, improve public safety, and promote state and local capacity and responsibility for flood management.

In WRDA 1986, consistent with the Commission's recommendations, Congress increased the nonfederal cost-share requirements for local Corps flood control and coastal storm projects from none at all to 35%. Bureau of Reclamation construction actions with flood control benefits, however, continue to be 100% non-reimbursable. How to fairly address and account for private gains from federal projects continues to be debated, with the private benefits and development incentives in flood- and erosion-prone coastal areas created by Corps beach replenishment receiving particular scrutiny. The 110th Congress, in WRDA 2007, called for the Secretary of the Army to update water resources planning guidance. The update is to be consistent with actions being justified solely on the basis of public benefits. How this provision, as well as other WRDA 2007 provisions related to a national policy for wise use of flood-prone areas, will be implemented remains unknown (See "Water Resources Project Planning and Evaluation" for more information).

Some of the more significant enacted changes in flood-related policy have consisted of efforts to improve the NFIP (e.g., improvements to increase participation in the program and better manage repetitive loss properties)[60] and reorganization of federal emergency response and recovery following the 9/11 attacks and Hurricane Katrina's impact on New Orleans. Considerable concerns continue to be raised about the degree of subsidization under the NFIP and the financial foundation of the program. Numerous Government Accountability Office (GAO) studies have reviewed various aspects of the NFIP; some of the recommendations have been implemented. In 2006, an independent review working group released its evaluation of the NFIP;[61] the recommendations are among other changes that have been considered, but not enacted, as part of recent NFIP legislation. Reorganization of emergency response, in particular the placement of FEMA within the Department of Homeland Security, remains a topic of much debate.

Hurricane Katrina, levee breaks in California and Nevada, and the 2008 Midwest floods have increased the recent debate about how to manage flood, coastal, and aging infrastructure risks, what is an acceptable level of risk—especially for low-probability, high-consequence events—and who should bear the costs to reduce these risks (particularly in the case of levees and coastal development). The policy issue is how to use limited fiscal resources to address a wide range of concerns, including protecting concentrated urban populations, reducing risk to the nation's public and private economic infrastructure, reducing vulnerability by investing in natural buffers, and equity in protection for low-income and minority populations. The challenge is how to structure actions and programs so they provide incentives to limit flood-prone lands to their best use; to tackle this challenge would require significant adjustments in the flood insurance program, disaster aid policies and practices, and programs for structural and nonstructural measures and actions, without infringing on private property rights or usurping local decision making. Hurricane Katrina also raised the sensitive question of whether and how federal agencies can raise concerns, particularly as they relate to public safety, about actions directed by Congress. In the early 1990s, Congress overrode the Corps' analysis of how to reduce flooding from hurricanes in New Orleans in favor of a locally preferred floodwall option;[62] these floodwalls were the site of significant failures during Hurricane Katrina.

Damage caused by Hurricane Katrina and other coastal storms illustrate the growing flood and erosion risks of the nation's coastal developments. Hurricane-prone states have increasingly dominated NFIP outlays. Since the mid-1960s, the federal role in hurricane storm protection also has become more prominent; the Corps, with nonfederal sponsors, builds structures and places sand periodically for beach renourishment to reduce flooding.

Hurricane Katrina also brought national attention to the issue of levee and floodwall reliability and different levels of protection provided by flood damage reduction structures—some of which were built by the federal government, but most of which have been constructed by local entities. Levee overtopping and failure contribute to approximately one-third of all flood disasters, and a large percentage of locally built levees are poorly designed and maintained. How to address levee reliability and various levels of protection is a current issue that did not receive much attention in the Commission's report. WRDA 2007 builds on some post-Katrina actions that supported developing a levee inventory; it requires the Corps to establish and maintain a database with an inventory of the nation's levees by 2009 and to inspect federally constructed and other levees. WRDA 2007 also created a National Committee on Levee Safety to make recommendations to Congress for a national levee safety program. It also requires Corps planning to consider the risk that remains behind levees and floodwalls, upstream and downstream impacts, and equitable analysis of structural and nonstructural alternatives. How these provisions and the recommendations by the National Committee on Levee Safety are implemented over the next few years may affect the nature of the federal and local investment in flood and storm damage infrastructure and mitigation measures.

Drought in many parts of the country also is drawing attention to options for capturing and treating urban stormwater as a potential water supply. Stormwater is increasingly being seen as a resource (e.g., for reuse), rather than only for its negative effects on water quality and urban flooding.

Estuaries and the Coastal Zone[63]

Estuaries—formed at the confluence of freshwater flows (e.g., rivers and streams) and the ocean—are considered some of the most biologically rich areas on earth. Many animal species rely on estuaries for habitat, especially for places to spawn or nest and for nurseries to support early life stages and juveniles. Human communities rely on estuaries and nearshore areas for direct benefits such as food and recreation and indirect benefits such as filters of pollutants and as buffers from floods and intense storms. Over half of the U.S. population now lives in coastal watershed counties.

Issue

The Commission found that the nation's estuaries and shorelands had been "subjected to massive physical modification, threatening the ecological balance and the maintenance of high biological productivity."[64] The Commission further noted that the federal government had played a large role in the physical modification of estuaries and shorelands, primarily through water resource projects undertaken by the Corps, as well as many federal agency activities in major river basins that empty into the nation's estuaries. For example, modifications on the Mississippi River, in part, have caused reduction of sediment load that is necessary for maintaining coastal wetlands in Louisiana; and agricultural pollution has reduced water quality in the Chesapeake Bay and along the Gulf Coast. The Commission found that decisions about where, whether, and how to dredge and fill waterways and harbors, develop real estate, preserve natural systems, locate industries, and dispose of wastes determine to a large extent the uses and health of the waters and shorelands of the coastal zone, including wetlands.

NWC Recommendations

An overarching NWC recommendation on estuaries and the coastal zone called for coastal zone planning to be handled in coordination with general land use and water resources planning at all levels of government. In addition, the Commission specifically recommended that:

- water resources and development plans should include measures to protect estuaries and coastal zones; and
- costs of protection should be included in project costs and borne by project beneficiaries, except when benefits are widespread, national in scope, or cannot be tied to beneficiaries.

Current Status and Implementation

Several pieces of legislation have been enacted and programs implemented to protect the coasts and estuaries since 1973. Coastal programs and legislation established since 1973 generally represent targeted treatment of estuaries and coastal zones; however, they do not represent an integration of coastal zone planning with general land use plans and broad water resource plans. The type of integration envisioned by the Commission was constrained by the contraction of large-scale water resource planning efforts in the 1980s.[65] Without these larger planning efforts, federal water resource projects are planned and evaluated largely as individual projects. Consequently, the cumulative impacts of multiple and existing projects in a basin or ecosystem on coastal and estuarine resources often are not fully examined. In contrast, the impacts of individual projects on estuarine and coastal resources generally are examined and environmental mitigation measures are developed during individual project planning. Mitigation costs are generally shared between the federal and nonfederal sponsor based on the primary purposes of the project.

Coastal Zone Management Program

Implementation of the Coastal Zone Management Program, established by the Coastal Zone Management Act of 1972[66] and the National Estuary Program (NEP), which was created in amendments to the CWA in 1987,[67] arguably have caused the most significant movement toward the Commission's recommendation that water resources and development plans protect coasts and estuaries, and be integrated with land use planning. The Coastal Zone Management Program supports the creation of state plans that encourage coastal development while protecting resources. The NEP focuses conservation, management, and restoration efforts on estuaries of national significance, many of them in proximity to coastal development (e.g., Puget Sound, which borders Seattle and Tacoma, WA). It currently covers 28 estuaries located throughout most of the coastal continental United States and Puerto Rico. The Chesapeake Bay Program, although not a part of the NEP, is managed by a similar approach with federal-state partnerships; the program develops and participating agencies implement plans to improve water quality. NEP programs have financed projects targeted at protecting and restoring habitat, conducting outreach, upgrading municipal stormwater infrastructure, and implementing other priority actions in their management plans.

Other Coastal Programs and Laws

Several other programs and laws are closely related to coastal zone management. For example, the Coastal Nonpoint Pollution Control Program, established by the Coastal Zone Act Reauthorization Amendments of 1990 (Section 6217 of P.L. 101-508; 16 U.S.C. 1455b), is intended to strengthen links between state coastal zone management and water quality programs by requiring coastal states to develop a nonpoint pollution control program to restore and protect coastal waters. Further, the Coastal and Estuarine Land Conservation Program (Title II of P.L. 107-77; 16 U.S.C. 1456d) provides matching grants to eligible states and local governments to acquire property or easements on coastal property. Projects have protected coastal habitats, reduced coastal water pollution, and improved access for coastal recreation.

The Coastal Barrier Resources Act, enacted in 1982 (16 U.S.C. 3501, et seq., P.L. 97-348), prohibits federal financing of development in areas designated as part of the coastal barrier system. The system includes 585 units and nearly 1.3 million acres of land and associated aquatic areas.

Trends Affecting the Coasts and Coastal Planning

Although coastal zone planning has expanded since 1973, the stress on coastal and estuarine ecosystems has not lessened as more intense development and population growth and increased water use have occurred in these sensitive environments. Some of the environmental consequences have worsened (e.g., expansion of the size and number of dead zones in coastal waters, especially the Gulf of Mexico). In 2004, the U.S. Commission on Ocean Policy noted that, as more people come to coastal areas to live, work, and visit, the nation has lost millions of acres of wetlands, seen the destruction of seagrass and kelp beds, and faced a significant loss of mangrove forests.[68]

The Commission focused largely on protection of estuaries and coasts. In some locations, water resources planning has moved beyond protecting these areas from incidental impacts associated with water resources projects. Restoration of estuaries, in particular, has become the core of a number of large-scale restoration planning efforts, such as the Chesapeake Bay, coastal Louisiana wetlands, and the California Bay-Delta. Aquatic ecosystem restoration has been added as a primary mission area for the Corps. The cost-share arrangements for these larger-scale efforts often are decided on a case-by-case basis, reflecting the uniqueness of each effort and of the federal responsibility in each effort.

One aspect of estuarine and coastal health that has received much policy attention since the Commission's report is coastal wetlands. Wetlands are critical to a clean, properly functioning environment and to ecosystem and species health. Federal data indicate that historic trends of inland wetland acreage loss due especially to urban and rural development have been substantially slowed and even slightly reversed nationally in recent years. A number of federal, state, and local programs involving regulation, protection, and conservation contribute to the recent national trend of net gain. However, the same trends are not occurring in coastal areas, where data indicate that coastal watersheds have been losing a substantial amount of wetlands and will continue to do so because of continuing development in those areas.[69]

Channelization[70]

Issue
The Commission identified the negative environmental effects of channelization—the straightening of streams—as an issue. It found that evaluations of channelization investments had given insufficient weight to environmental harm from channelization relative to channelization's drainage, flood control, navigation, and erosion control benefits. The Commission found that evaluation tools often ignored or underestimated negative effects on groundwater infiltration, fish and wildlife habitat, downstream sedimentation and flooding, and aesthetic value.

NWC Recommendations
The Commission recommended:

- improvements to the evaluation procedures in channelization plans;
- a user pay approach for costs that increase the value of private lands; and
- review of probable effects of already authorized channelization plans, and provision of funds only to those with national benefits exceeding all costs.

Current Status and Implementation
Since the Commission's report, most federal channelization efforts, such as those at USDA and the Corps, have been abolished or gone unfunded. Some plans using channelization are still developed as components of flood damage reduction, navigation, and other federal projects. For these efforts, the detrimental effects of channelization are evaluated and addressed pursuant to federal and state environmental laws, fish and wildlife mitigation requirements, and species protection measures. The dredged material produced during construction and maintenance of channels previously was disposed as waste; now, it is often put to beneficial environmental use, such as island building and wetland restoration. (See also "Water Resources Project Planning and Evaluation.")

Fish and Wildlife Protection[71]

Issue

The Commission found that water projects often had been planned and developed with little regard for fish and wildlife impacts, resulting in harm to these resources. Specifically, it noted:

> [t]housands of miles of natural stream channels were relocated or altered; some streams were dried up; estuaries and marshes suffered from drainage and landfill operations; and estuarine habitat essential for shellfish and other species was destroyed by dredging and channel deepening. Water quality deterioration and water temperature alteration have also adversely affected fish and wildlife resources in both marine and fresh waters.[72]

The Commission expressed concern that state and federal legislation at the time might not fully address these impacts. However, the NWC found that federal protections under the Fish and Wildlife Coordination Act (FWCA; Act of March 10, 1934, as amended (16 U.S.C. §§661- 666(e)) and NEPA "seem to be adequate to prevent unreasonable or unnecessary damage to [fish and wildlife] resources under future projects constructed or licensed by the Federal Government."[73]

NWC Recommendations

To better address fish and wildlife impacts, the Commission recommended that fish and wildlife agencies jointly participate in initial water project planning, as opposed to reacting at later stages. The NWC argued that the FWCA requires this collaboration, and that this collaboration should be continued and strengthened. The Commission also was concerned that the FWCA did not cover nonfederal entities. It recommended that all states enact legislation to protect fish and wildlife resources from impacts of nonfederal water projects. The Commission recommended having the WRC supervise and coordinate the resolution of stakeholder disagreements.

NEPA also was a concern for the NWC because, in 1973, implementation of NEPA was just beginning. The Commission also called for more research and data on the effects of water projects on fish and wildlife, and for steps to reduce water-related conflicts by reducing uncertainty and producing scientifically defensible results.

Current Status and Implementation

Water resources planning and project development practices now give significantly more attention to fish and wildlife than in 1973. Many of the fish and wildlife accomplishments have been achieved through wetlands conservation under the CWA, fish and wildlife agency consultation pursuant to ESA,[74] assessment requirements of NEPA, and site specific legislation.[75] Federal fish and wildlife agencies still appear largely to operate in a reactive mode, responding to plans already formulated and when species have already declined to low levels. In sum, improvements have been made, but the sufficiency of these improvements is debated. The NWC may have contributed to improvements, but indirectly.

Today, there are many more threats to fish and wildlife resources than impacts from federal water project development. These threats include destruction of habitat due to other development, invasive non-native species, climate variability and change, and pollution. Despite past achievements, fish and wildlife resources continue to decline. Specifically, the FWS notes that "aquatic resources in the United States are in decline, and habitat destruction and modification are the principal culprits."[76]

Application of the FWCA

Consistent with the NWC recommendation, attempts were made to establish regulations to implement the FWCA in the late 1970s and early 1980s, but they were abandoned during the Reagan Administration.[77] FWCA currently is applied to water activities through each agency's planning process. For example, the Corps and Reclamation consider FWCA requirements when preparing NEPA documentation. However, FWCA, like NEPA, imposes procedural requirements, not substantive obligations on the "action agency" to avoid adverse affects on fish and wildlife. According to one source, the FWCA has "largely [been] overshadowed by NEPA, and undercut by a series of disabling judicial interpretations. Its promise, once viewed with considerable optimism, remains largely unfulfilled."[78] The role of WRC as arbitrator became moot when this coordination mechanism was disbanded in 1983.

Research on Water Resource Project Impacts on Fish

The NWC recommendation supporting more fish and wildlife research at a national level has not been implemented. There is, however, greater understanding than existed in 1973 of how certain types of water projects such as reservoirs can affect fisheries and other species. For example, in the Columbia River Basin, considerable research has been done on the effects of water infrastructure on fisheries and habitat.[79] Similarly, much research has been done on fisheries affected by Reclamation projects in California and elsewhere.

As the NWC predicted, fish and wildlife data are central to several current conflicts. Insufficient scientific understanding of when, how much, and the quality of the water needed to sustain fisheries and habitat, and how this affects the quantity available for water supply, continues to plague some conflicts and at times is used to support delay in protections for fish and wildlife.

State Protection of Fish and Wildlife Values on Nonfederal Waters

The Commission recommended that states provide protection for fish and wildlife resources on non-federally managed waters, similar to the FWCA on federal projects. Analyzing state programs and resources for conserving and protecting fish and wildlife in detail is beyond the scope of this report.[80] State efforts, however, are aided by federal programs, some of which have been strengthened since 1973. For example, amendments enacted in 1984 (also known as Wallop- Breaux or Dingell-Johnson Act; 16 U.S.C. 777, et seq.) increased the funds available via the Federal Aid in Sport Fish Restoration Act of 1950, by extending its tax to a wider set of sporting equipment; this increased the amount of funding available to assist states in carrying out projects for management of sport fishery resources, conservation, and restoration.[81]

"USERS PAY" OR "BENEFICIARY PAYS" APPROACH

General Water Resource User Fee and Cost-Share Policies[82]

Issue

Chapter 15 identified a host of negative effects associated with what the Commission termed "deficiencies" in federal cost-share policies. Taken together, effects of the identified deficiencies can best be described as inefficiencies in federal water resources management. Specific federal cost-share issues identified by the Commission include:

- inconsistencies among cost-share policies within certain agencies for accomplishing similar purposes (e.g., different cost-share policies for

Corps of Engineers' federal flood control reservoirs, levees, and floodwalls);

- inconsistency in cost-share policies across federal agencies for similar projects (e.g., different policies and repayment schemes for Corps, NRCS, and Reclamation water supply projects);
- non-uniform repayment terms for nonfederal cost shares;
- lack of taxpayer equity due to favorable cost-share and/or repayment mechanisms for nonfederal project beneficiaries; and
- unnecessary expansion of the federal role (and cost) in water resource development, and project development without "compelling social purpose" at federal expense.

The negative effects of these issues were found to be numerous. For example, the Commission noted that inconsistent federal flood control policies (in contemporary terms known as flood risk or flood damage reduction policies) resulted in some types of flood projects being favored financially by local sponsors over others, even though another approach might be more economically or technically efficient or effective.[83] Similarly, different cost-share policies across federal agencies were found to result in confusion, distortion of best approaches to resolve problems, and in local sponsors "shopping around" the agencies for the best financial deal. The Commission also found that non-uniform repayment terms for construction costs resulted in misallocation of taxpayer resources, and that differences in discount rates used to evaluate projects and interest rates used for repayment purposes also resulted in inefficiencies. Additionally, the Commission noted that overly favorable cost-share policies resulted in project beneficiaries seeking projects they were unwilling to pay for without federal support, which in turn led to "unwise" development in areas "prone to periodic flooding and hurricane hazards." Finally, the Commission contended that easily accessible favorable cost-share policies had led "in many instances to Federal construction of projects that could just as well have been built by nonfederal interests" resulting in an unnecessary expansion of the federal role and a tendency "to move control over water resources to Washington officials" at increasing federal expense.[84]

NWC Recommendations

The Commission recommended many changes in federal cost-share policies. Specific recommendations include recovery of federal costs and ensuring that project beneficiaries pay proportional development and operating costs for water programs or activities. The recommendations are too numerous and context-specific to address in this analysis; however, a few major topics (inland navigation, irrigation water supply, and municipal water and wastewater treatment) are discussed in separate sections below. In addition, the Commission also made other, more general, recommendations that better lend themselves to analysis in today's context. The following more general recommendations were offered by the Commission:

- establish uniform cost-share policies for all alternatives for a given water purpose (e.g., for different approaches, such as levees, floodwalls, flood storage reservoirs, and nonstructural measures);
- allow agencies to broaden the scope of what is an acceptable project or alternative (e.g., relocation of floodplain communities, conjunctive use of surface and groundwater supplies);
- establish uniform or consistent cost-share policies across federal agencies (i.e., Corps, Reclamation, and NRCS should have same cost-share policies for water supply and flood damage reduction projects);
- utilize interagency coordination mechanisms to "channel" water project applications to a single agency for negotiation;[85]
- require uniformity in the cost share embedded in construction cost repayment mechanisms;
- require use of the same discount and interest rates for project evaluation and repayment (an interest rate reflecting the yield on long-term U.S. bonds);
- charge interest during construction and development (i.e., eliminate interest-free development periods);
- establish "beneficiary pays" payment systems through pricing and charges (i.e., taxes, special assessments, and fees); and
- ensure that direct project beneficiaries pay all costs of projects unless there is some social benefit to a federal "subsidy."

Overall, the Commission concluded that "appropriate cost-sharing policies should provide incentives for the development of efficient projects in harmony with other National programs and policies."[86] Other chapters repeated this overarching theme of users pay—or beneficiary pays. (See "Inland Waterway User Charges," "Federal Irrigation Policy—Reclamation Reform," and "Pricing of Municipal and Industrial Water and Wastewater Services," below.)

Current Status and Implementation

Some "users pay" changes consistent with the Commission report were adopted in the late 1970s and 1980s (e.g., Reclamation reform, and transportation cost share changes in WRDA 1986); however, they did not come easily. Disagreement over whether and how to raise the local cost share for Corps projects held up authorizations from the mid-1970s until 1986.[87] Similar disagreements occurred over increasing prices or repayment policies for irrigation programs. Concerns over appropriate levels of nonfederal and federal cost share, their consistency across agencies and water resource purposes, and their effect on other important federal policies, remain today.

While some cost-share issues identified by the Commission were addressed in WRDA 1986, consistency in federal financing has not been achieved. Cost-share policies for the Corps and Reclamation flood projects differ. The agencies also differ significantly in financing for irrigation water supply. Standardization of cost shares across the projects of an agency also has not been maintained, primarily due to the continued congressional practice of authorizing individual projects.

Although several actions have been attempted to address inconsistencies in federal financing, WRDA 1986 was perhaps the most fundamental accomplishment in this area. It contained several incremental changes in Corps cost-share policies and established limited local sponsor requirements—most notably for deep draft navigation, inland waterways, and flood control—but contained few incentives for lower-cost, nonstructural alternatives for flood control. Other efforts to address cost-share issues and adequate assessment of benefits and costs included the 1977 Carter water plan and the development of Principles and Standards for project evaluation (later Principles and Guidelines). These efforts were ultimately abandoned or overtaken by other events. (See also "Water Resources Project Planning and Evaluation" for information on assessment of project benefits and costs and discussion of consistent planning evaluation and selection.)

In sum, the determination of appropriate cost shares for federal water resource projects, and to some degree for water quality infrastructure, continues to be an issue in federal water policy and management. While it may be an efficient way to allocate scarce federal resources, instituting "beneficiary pays" or "users pay" fee policies remains difficult politically.

Inland Waterway User Charges[88]

Twelve thousand miles of commercially active U.S. inland and intracoastal waterways support barge traffic carrying roughly 15% of the national volume of intercity cargo. Coal, petroleum, farm products, chemicals, minerals, and aggregates for construction are the primary products carried on the inland waterway system.

Issue

The Commission found that, while federal funding of the inland waterway system was appropriate as a means to encouraging settlement and economic activity in regions served, these goals had been achieved. It concluded that identifiable users of the inland waterway system should bear its costs. The Commission argued that this would be more efficient, that is freight would be allocated to its true least-cost transportation mode, rather than freight being diverted to modes with greater federal support. The Commission's recommendation was not a new idea; legislation proposing the same changes had been introduced since the 1930s, and many administrations, beginning with Roosevelt in 1940, have advocated for waterway user charges.[89]

NWC Recommendations

The Commission recommended that inland waterway users, both freight and pleasure craft, be charged a user fee set to recover all operation and maintenance costs. The Commission recommended a uniform fuel tax plus a lockage fee to be phased in over ten years. Regarding new inland waterway construction, the Commission recommended that project beneficiaries also repay the full cost over a period of years unless the national defense benefits of the project justified some federal cost share.[90]

Current Status and Implementation

Congress has enacted an inland waterway user fee that recovers about one-tenth of the federal cost associated with the system. Efforts supporting a full cost-recovery user fee have failed.

Partial User Charges Enacted

Congress only partially acted on the Commission's recommendations for inland waterway user charges: the current user charge scheme consists only of a fuel tax; does not include lockage fees; is only imposed on freight barges and not pleasure craft; and the fuel tax recovers only 10% of the federal costs associated with the inland waterway system, rather than recovering 100% of the costs.[91] In 1978, Congress enacted the Inland Waterways Revenue Act (P.L. 95-502, §202; 26 U.S.C. 4042) which imposed a 4 cents per gallon fuel tax on freight barges beginning in 1980, with a gradual increase to 10 cents per gallon beginning in 1985. These fuel taxes were to be deposited in an Inland Waterway Trust Fund (IWTF) and used to pay for a portion of the federal cost of new construction and major rehabilitation projects. With each project authorization, Congress decides what portion of the cost will be paid with General Funds versus IWTF monies, but the split thus far has generally been 50-50. All operation and maintenance costs on the inland waterway system are funded with General Funds. In WRDA 1986 (P.L. 99-662, § 1404), Congress imposed another gradual rate increase in the fuel tax over a five-year period, from 11 cents per gallon beginning in 1990 to 20 cents per gallon beginning in 1995. The current tax rate is 20 cents per gallon.

Congressional Resistance to Full Cost-Recovery User Charges

Congress has resisted attempts to raise inland waterway user charges.[92] Congress considered a nearly full-cost recovery proposal before enacting the 1978 Act. Senator Domenici's initial proposal (S. 790, 95th Congress) called for a system of tolls and license fees raising about $200 million per year to recover 100% of the Corps operations and maintenance expenses on the inland waterways and half of the construction expenses. The Carter Administration advocated for a 42 cent per gallon fuel tax, which was thought to be the rate needed to raise the same amount. The railroads suggested a tax of 64 cents per gallon, while the barge industry suggested a one cent per gallon charge. The barge industry supported the fuel tax bill because the bill also authorized replacement of Lock and Dam 26 on the Mississippi River at Alton, Illinois, a long-standing industry priority.[93] When Congress enacted a 10 cent increase in the fuel tax over a five year period in the 1986 act, it once again debated the level of user fees.[94]

Equity and economic arguments can be made for imposing a full cost-recovery user fee. As the 1973 Commission argued, inequities among freight modes in the provision of infrastructure diverts cargo to the most subsidized mode. The rail and pipeline industries, which compete with the barge industry for large shipments of dry and liquid bulk commodities, finance their infrastructure without public funds. The trucking industry, which competes with the barge industry in certain segments, pays fuel and other taxes into the Highway Trust Fund; these user fees for the heaviest trucks cover 50%-80% of their infrastructure costs.[95] If barge rates are subsidized, the nation incurs a higher overall cost for freight. The inequity also extends to shippers. If bulk and other commodity producers with access to barge transport can ship at artificially low prices, it could retard the production of these goods in regions without waterway access. A second efficiency argument for increasing user charges is that waterway users will demand that their contributions be spent on investments with the greatest economic returns.

The Commission recommended a lockage fee in addition to a uniform fuel tax to account for the fact that long segments of waterways, like the lower Mississippi River, have no need for locks. Because the present fee is uniform on all inland waterways, cross-subsidization takes place between heavily used waterways with relatively low infrastructure costs to lightly used waterways with relatively high costs. It can be argued that this is appropriate within a waterway network like the Mississippi system, where branch waterways feed traffic into main channels, but the argument does not hold across disparate waterways that do not share traffic, such as the Columbia/Snake River system and the Mississippi system.

Continued consolidation of the barge industry, in which some companies are owned by or affiliated with large agricultural and energy product conglomerates (such as Archer Daniels Midland, Cargill, American Electric Power, and Marathon Ashland), has raised the ire of taxpayer groups, asking why these major corporations need continued public assistance in the form of heavily subsidized waterways. The barge industry notes that they are the only waterway users that pay a fee. Other beneficiaries of the system, such as recreational users, do not share in the cost.

In addition to the 1973 Commission report, many economic studies have evaluated and analyzed the trade-offs among alternative user charge schemes, such as system-wide versus segment-specific fees, annual license fees versus per-use fees, congestion tolls, lockage fees, per ton-mile fees, and combinations of these alternatives.[96] While economic and equity arguments can be made for increasing the share of costs borne by waterway users, Congress has thus far not been persuaded to increase fees beyond what was accomplished in WRDA 1986.

Federal Irrigation Policy—Reclamation Reform[97]

The Reclamation Act of 1902 authorized the construction of projects to provide water for irrigation in western states. Pursuant to the act, as amended,

Reclamation (Department of the Interior) has built and now manages hundreds of dams, canals, and related facilities in 17 western states. Overall, these facilities serve a population of approximately 31 million, delivering a total of nearly 30 million acre-feet of water annually (an acre foot is enough to cover one acre of land one foot deep, or 325,851 gallons) for agricultural and municipal and industrial (M&I) use.

Originally, Reclamation projects were to be financed through the sale of public lands; however, early on, this funding source proved to be too limited to support the Reclamation program. Instead, Reclamation projects historically have been constructed with federal funds, with water and power users entering contracts to "reimburse" or "repay" the federal government for the portion of construction costs that can be allocated to different project purposes. Repayment requirements are typically 100% of federal costs, with interest, for M&I users; repayment requirements are generally 100%, with no interest, for agricultural users, unless repayment is reduced per users' "ability-to-pay." Further, to avoid land and resource speculation, the original act limited to 160 acres the amount of land any one person could own and still receive reclamation water (known as the 160-acre limit, or acreage limitation).

Issue

The Commission identified the Bureau of Reclamation's irrigation program as one of several programs contributing to inefficient water management. It found that irrigation subsidies and antiquated residency and ownership requirements inefficiently allocated water supplies in the West. The Commission cited population pressures, fish and wildlife needs, and surplus agricultural production as reasons for reexamination of the Reclamation irrigation program.

NWC Recommendations

The Commission made several recommendations related to Reclamation's irrigation program. These recommendations were aimed largely at reducing irrigation interest subsidies and eliminating or reducing the acreage limit. In the Commission's view, these changes would increased economic and water allocation efficiencies in the Reclamation program.

With respect to authorization of *future* irrigation projects, the Commission recommended that:

- new irrigation projects should not be subsidized as in the past;

- direct beneficiaries of irrigation projects should pay the full costs of new projects; and
- Congress should abolish the (then-existing) 160-acre land ownership limit for new projects, provided that direct beneficiaries pay full irrigation construction costs.

The Commission also recommended that for *existing* Reclamation projects, Congress enact legislation to exempt irrigation districts and landowners from the 160-acre limitation. It further recommended that Congress authorize several actions, including the following:

- a lump-sum payment on irrigation repayment obligations;
- payment of interest on remaining irrigation repayment obligations;
- retention of land above the limit (excess acreage) if a landowner formally agrees to sell excess acreage and makes a lump-sum payment or pays interest on costs assigned to all land owned, including the original 160 acres; and
- use of project water on new acquisitions of excess acreage if new owners make a lump-sum payment or pay interest on costs assigned to all land owned, including the original 160 acres.

Current Status and Implementation
The Commission's recommendation for a reduction of irrigation subsidies and the linkage of this recommendation to acreage limitation were addressed in part via Reclamation legislation in 1982 and 1992, as discussed below. These recommendations, which were to become known as "Reclamation reform," were among the report's most controversial proposals. Almost immediately upon release of the NWC's draft report, and upon its final release in June of 1973, several Members of Congress denounced these recommendations. Most of their statements argued that such changes would have disastrous effects on irrigators in the West and the nation's food supply. There was support, however, for change in some quarters. Specific challenges to the program were epitomized by a series of lawsuits against Reclamation for its implementation of the excess acreage provisions of reclamation law, beginning in the mid-1970s.[98] Counter lawsuits also ensued.

Partial Reclamation Reforms Enacted

Congress enacted Reclamation reform legislation in 1982, and made further attempts at reforming the reclamation program in the late 1980s and early 1990s.

1982 Reclamation Reform Act. Congress enacted the Reclamation Reform Act of 1982 (RRA; P.L. 97-293, 43 U.S.C. 390aa) after several years of administrative review and congressional oversight of reclamation acreage limitation and irrigation subsidy issues.[99] The RRA directly addresses some of the acreage limitation issues and in part addresses the interest subsidy issues raised by the Commission. In particular, the RRA increases the acreage limitation for water districts and water users who chose to comply with the new law, while allowing others to remain under "prior law." For those electing to comply with the new law, the acreage limit was raised from 160 acres under the original 1902 Reclamation Act to 960 acres for individuals and groups of 25 or less, and 640 acres for legal entities benefitting more than 25 persons.

The RRA also addresses the interest rate subsidy in part by establishing a penalty for individuals and entities electing to remain under prior law. Those remaining under prior law are to be charged "full cost" for reclamation water delivered to land leased in excess of 160 acres. Full cost is defined within the act as the allocable irrigation capital repayment obligation and any operations and maintenance deficit, plus interest on both accruing from the date of RRA enactment. This provision (Section 203(b)) is popularly known as the "hammer clause." Additionally, recognizing the complex ownership, landholding, and farm operations arrangements, some reclamation water users had used to effectively extend the delivery of water to more than 160 acres, the RRA also includes provisions charging full cost for water delivered to landholdings above the new acre limit. Finally, Section 213 of the RRA explicitly provides that the ownership and full cost pricing limitations would not apply to project lands after irrigation repayment obligations have been meet, including under lump sum or accelerated payments.

One could argue that Congress took steps to address the recommendations of the Commission regarding linking increases in acreage limits to increased fees for reclamation water; however, one could also argue that the Commission's vision of a simplified reclamation program based on elimination of the acre limit for efficiency's sake and for better allocation of water via pricing became much more complex and cumbersome under the RRA.

1990s Reclamation Reform. Further attempts by Congress to address acreage limitation and irrigation subsidy issues were made in the late 1980s and early 1990s. "Reclamation reform" bills were introduced and debated, as was legislation to address the use of interest-free Reclamation water on "surplus crops"—crops deemed to be in surplus by the U.S. Department of Agriculture and for which growers receive commodity payments under USDA programs. Reclamation reform provisions were eventually dropped from omnibus reclamation legislation in the 102nd Congress when compromise language was reached on "reform" of Reclamation policy related to the Central Valley Project (CVP) in California—the Central Valley Project Improvement Act (CVPIA; Title 34 of P.L. 102-575; 106 Stat. 4600). Some new pricing provisions were included in CVPIA, as well as new fees to support fish and wildlife restoration and mitigation; however, these provisions apply only to the CVP. Tiered water pricing provisions of the CVPIA—intended to encourage water conservation—remain particularly controversial.

In sum, while Congress addressed some aspects of both acreage limitation and the interest subsidy in 1982, these issues remain "third-rail" policy issues when it comes to Reclamation oversight. For example, 25 years after the 1973 NWC report, the Western Water Policy Review Advisory Commission made similar recommendations regarding recouping taxpayer investments and instituting something closer to full cost pricing. These recommendations met with stiff opposition from key Members of Congress and were criticized by the then-Chairman of the Senate Appropriations Committee, Senator Ted Stevens, and the then-Chairman of the House Resources Committee, Rep. Don Young, as "decidedly biased against irrigated agriculture" and commodity production."[100] Congress has not directly addressed these issues since attempts in the early 1990s to amend the RRA to address circumvention of the acreage limitation provisions of reclamation law and project beneficiary receipt of dual water and crop "subsidies."

Pricing of Municipal and Industrial Water and Wastewater Services[101]

Appropriate pricing of municipal and industrial water and wastewater services was an issue before publication of the NWC report and continues to be debated. Research and case studies indicate that both rate structure and rate level can encourage more efficient water use. At the federal level, the CWA requires that utility recipients of federal assistance for capital projects charge user fees covering the full costs of operation, maintenance, and replacement, but does not dictate local utility rates and charges. These are matters under the jurisdiction of state or local regulatory authorities.

Issue and NWC Recommendations

The Commission addressed the important role of full cost pricing and user charges in the delivery of water and sewer services to customers. It noted that proper pricing would conserve scarce water supplies, discourage or delay investment in water infrastructure projects, and make the use of resources more efficient. The Commission recognized that utility regulation may be aimed at accomplishing multiple objectives, and only incidentally be concerned with conserving and efficiently using water supplies. Still, it recommended that water and sewerage charges should be based on the costs that users impose upon the system and the costs imposed on society from the loss of the use of the resource for other purposes.

Current Status and Implementation

According to available information, water utilities and systems vary widely in adoption of conservation- or efficiency-oriented rate and pricing policies. The issue remains a concern for federal policymakers, as reflected in the fact that the Senate Environment and Public Works Committee approved legislation (S. 3500, 110th Congress) with a provision calling for a study by the National Academy of Sciences on cost of service. Among other topics, the study would determine whether rates set by U.S. public water systems and waste treatment works were established using a full-cost pricing model; would identify a set of best industry practices for use in establishing rates structures that address full cost of service and water conservation while taking into consideration disadvantaged individuals and communities; and assess the extent to which affordability affects the decision of a utility to increase rates.

IMPROVEMENTS TO WATER QUALITY

Water Pollution Control[102]

Issue

The Commission made a number of recommendations related to water pollution control. Initially, the Commission identified the range of sources then contributing to U.S. water quality impairments—municipal sewage, industrial wastes, stormwater runoff, animal wastes from commercial feedlots, and nonpoint sources (sediment, chemicals and fertilizers, abandoned mine drainage). It noted that existing monitoring and surveillance programs were inadequate to provide the data required for a comprehensive analysis of water quality conditions. Nevertheless, water quality trends, drawn from available data, showed a mixed picture, with water quality improving in some areas but deteriorating elsewhere.

These observations could just as well be made today. Considerable progress has been made toward improving water quality, especially in controlling conventional pollutants (suspended solids, bacteria, and oxygen-consuming materials) discharged by industries and sewage treatment plants. However, progress has been mixed in controlling discharges of toxic pollutants (heavy metals, inorganic and organic chemicals), which are more numerous and can harm human health and the environment even when present in very small amounts. Nonpoint sources of pollution are believed to be responsible for the majority of water quality impairments nationwide. Overall, data reported by the Environmental Protection Agency (EPA) and states indicate that 45% of river and stream miles assessed by states and 47% of assessed lake acres do not meet applicable standards and are impaired for one or more desired uses.[103]

NWC Recommendations, and Current Status and Implementation

The Commission's recommendations covered several areas: Clean Water Act (CWA) goals; water quality standards; subsidies and other economic inducements; planning; and federal and state roles.

Many of these recommendations have been addressed through implementation of the CWA; however, some concerns identified by the Commission remain valid today.[104]

The water pollution chapter was controversial at the time because it rejected some of the fundamental concepts that Congress had recently adopted in the 1972 Federal Water Pollution Control Act Amendments (FWPCA; P.L. 92-500, also commonly referred to as the CWA), especially the zero discharge goal and the core regulatory approach of the legislation, which remain central to the law. The CWA is viewed today as one of the most successful environmental laws in terms of achieving its statutory goals, which have been widely supported by the public. The Commission made observations that remain valid about the extent of water pollution problems, despite water quality improvements that have occurred since then. Issues on which the

Commission focused some recommendations, such as planning, federal and state roles, and enforcement through discharge permits, have been and remain basic elements of implementing water quality programs. The need to adequately fund pollution control activities, highlighted in several recommendations, also remains a challenge for policymakers.

Clean Water Act Goals

The Commission acknowledged that decisive action was needed to shift away from water development to water quality management in order to achieve the nation's water quality objectives and meet a high standard of water quality. Nevertheless, the Commission rejected the ultimate objective of the 1972 FWPCA amendments, namely, the goal of zero discharge of pollutants into the nation's waters by 1985. The Commission termed this goal unrealistic and unsound and recommended that cleanup requirements should be based on local water use designations and water quality standards. Absolutely pure water is not necessary for many uses, it said. Moreover, the Commission rejected the core regulatory premise of the 1972 act, which requires that all industrial and municipal dischargers achieve minimum technology-based pollution control performance standards in order to accelerate water quality improvements nationwide. It favored tailoring requirements according to an analysis of the social and economic benefits and costs of compliance.

The fundamental policy and programmatic approach to water pollution control adopted in P.L. 92-500 remains central to the CWA. A National Commission on Water Quality, established by Congress in P.L. 92-500 to assess early implementation of the law, generally endorsed the overall approach of the 1972 law while recommending that Congress redefine the goal of zero discharge of pollutants by 1985 to stress conservation and reuse of resources, while also striving to achieve the act's objective of restoring and maintaining the chemical, physical, and biological integrity of the nation's waters.[105] The zero discharge goal was not attained by 1985, nor has it been achieved since then. Neither was the statutory goal modified or removed from the law; as an aspirational objective, "zero discharge of pollutants" remains in place.

Water Quality Standards

Rather than basing cleanup requirements on nationally uniform performance standards of waste removal[106] and a goal of zero discharge of pollutants, the Commission said that the goal of water pollution control programs should be to regulate human-induced alteration of water quality to achieve and maintain a quality sufficient to sustain the uses people wish to make of the water now or in the future. Thus, the Commission urged reliance on water quality standards as the basis for pollution control requirements.[107] However, this recommendation would have reversed the policy approach that Congress had just enacted in the 1972 FWPCA amendments and returned to the policy that had prevailed prior to then. Prior to P.L. 92-500, federal law required the development of water quality standards for interstate waters, and such standards were to be used to determine actual pollution levels and to allocate pollution reductions. However, assigning waste loads among all dischargers within a stream segment was an immense technical and scientific exercise that seriously hampered regulatory and enforcement actions. By 1972, there was a widespread perception that the water quality standards approach was flawed and that a tougher set of standards and enforcement procedures should be developed.

The Commission apparently assumed that the new statutory approach based on performance standards meant that water quality standards would no longer have a role in pollution control decisions, but that assumption was incorrect then and now. In fact, Congress intended that water quality standards would remain the backbone of such decisions, and so they have.[108] Once industrial and municipal dischargers achieve minimum nationally uniform performance standards, water quality standards determine where additional pollution controls are required to attain and protect designated water uses. Again, the National Commission on Water Quality established pursuant to P.L. 92-500 endorsed the law's regulatory approach of requiring minimum performance standards and relying on water quality standards as backup to establish more stringent pollution control limits, where necessary to meet stringent water uses. Today, these types of water quality-based requirements are central to program implementation.

Subsidies and Other Economic Inducements

The chapter mentioned several types of economic inducements that could be used to encourage pollution control activities (such as tax incentives, R&D grants to industries, and loans), but focused on subsidies for municipal wastewater treatment—that is, the CWA's construction grants program. The Commission was generally skeptical about subsidies that distort good local decision-making by removing the investment burden from the local level and that can blur important cost-benefit decisions. However, it said that for municipal wastewater treatment, subsidies in the form of grants to communities to construct sewage treatment plants are appropriate, where the national interest finds that necessary in order to achieve clean water on a national scale within a relatively short time. P.L. 92-500 greatly expanded what previously had been a fairly small program of grants to aid construction of municipal sewage treatment plants.[109] The federal assistance effort should terminate after 10 years, according to the Commission. It recommended that Congress provide $13 billion per year for 10 years and that after 1983, state and local governments should bear all responsibility to build, operate, and maintain wastewater treatment facilities.

Federal subsidies have continued long after the termination date that the Commission recommended. Moreover, Congress never provided the level of funding in any single year that the Commission recommended; the highest in any single year was $4.5 billion in 1978. Nationally, estimated funding needs for water quality projects remain very large (more than $200 billion), and an end to federal financial assistance seems unlikely soon.

The grants program continued through 1989, and it has now been replaced by a revolving loan fund program in which the federal government provides seed money to states, states make loans to communities for needed projects, and communities repay loans to states. This shift from a grant program to loans provides a smaller subsidy and is less economically distorting than the subsidized grant program that the Commission recommended be limited in duration. The issue of how large the federal assistance role should be and how long it should continue remains contentious.

Planning

Much of the discussion and several recommendations in the pollution control chapter emphasized planning. Planning too often has a narrow focus, the Commission said. To be effective, planning must be done on a regional or areawide basis, ideally incorporating water quality, water supply, other resource planning, and land use planning. The Commission recommended that expanded planning of regional water quality management be coordinated with planning carried out by the WRC and river basin commissions (under the Water Resources Planning Act) and that there be a major investment in water quality planning.

From a water quality perspective, the CWA contains several planning mechanisms. One is the so-called 208 program, which the National Water Commission endorsed because it called for waste management planning to be done comprehensively and on a larger scale than purely local bases. Although that planning effort was not implemented as the Commission (and others) anticipated or hoped, more important today in this context is the act's requirement that states carry out a continuing planning process (CWA Section 303(e)). The Commission's recommendation that water quality planning take place in coordination with the WRC did not occur and, of course, the Council no longer exists. States today are at the forefront in establishing long-term water management plans for the protection and development of the resources under their jurisdiction. Typically, these plans are developed in close consultation with regional or local agencies of the states.

Federal and State Roles

The Commission advocated shared federal and state responsibility for designing and implementing water pollution control policy, with the federal government establishing national policy, and states (and localities) carrying out day-to-day implementation. The level of government closest to a problem should deal with it, if competent to do so. In fact, a cooperative partnership among governmental levels is precisely what the CWA envisioned, and it is the system that has operated in practice for more than 35 years (despite some inevitable friction at times).

Monitoring. The Commission identified a need for vigorous monitoring and data collection to aid understanding of water quality trends and to inform better decisions in the future. The Commission saw roles for all levels of government in this effort, and it particularly recommended a major role for the U.S. Geological Survey (USGS) through a comprehensive water quality monitoring surveillance network.

Few would disagree with or reject a recommendation for more and better water quality monitoring, even today. Monitoring activities today are carried out by all levels of government and nongovernmental entities, and USGS oversees a national surveillance network and many specific programs and projects. Information gleaned from these data are used to inform policymakers and the public about the status and trends of water quality. Still, environmental monitoring generally, and water quality monitoring specifically, receive less priority and funding than do regulatory or capital improvement programs.

Research and Development. The Commission also identified needs for research in several areas, such as technology development, alternative waste treatment and disposal methods, and methods of controlling nonpoint sources of pollution. As with the preceding issue, few would disagree with or reject a recommendation for more and better research, today as in 1973. Similarly, resources and manpower allocated to research and development—especially applied R&D— historically have had low priority and been underfunded.

Adequate Funding. The Commission said that whatever goals are adopted, Congress and the President should be prepared to fully fund all activities. Similarly, states and localities should fully fund their activities, the Commission said. Shortages of adequate resources are a chronic problem for implementation of public policies.

Other NWC Recommendations

The Commission made a number of other observations and related recommendations in areas that were fully addressed in the 1972 FWPCA and have been integral to CWA programs since then (for example, requiring that federal wastewater treatment construction grants be contingent on adoption of local user charges, and utilizing uniform enforceable discharge permits to impose facility-specific pollution limits). It is unclear why these issues drew the Commission's attention, unless the Commission anticipated that the new statutory provisions would not be implemented.

WATER RIGHTS

Non-Indian Water Rights[110]

Water rights traditionally are regulated by states, rather than the federal government. Depending on individual state resources and historic development, it may use one of three water rights doctrines: riparian, prior appropriation, or a hybrid of the two. Under the riparian doctrine, a person who owns land that borders a watercourse has the right to make reasonable use of the water on that land.[111] Traditionally, users in the riparian system are limited only by the requirement of reasonableness in comparison to other users. Under the prior appropriation doctrine, a person who diverts water from a watercourse (regardless of his location relative thereto) and makes reasonable and beneficial use of the water may acquire a right to use of the water.[112] Typically, under a prior appropriation system of water rights, users apply for a permit from a state administrative agency which manages the acquisition and transfers of such rights. The prior appropriation system limits users to the quantified amount of water the user secured under the permit process with a priority based on the date the water right was conferred by the state. Because of this priority system, appropriative rights are often referred to by the phrase "first in time, first in right." Some states have implemented a dual system of water rights, assigning rights under both doctrines.

Generally speaking, states east of the Mississippi River follow a riparian doctrine of water rights, while western states follow the appropriation doctrine; however, some western states have hybrid systems. The distinction between appropriation and riparian doctrines arises primarily from the historic availability of water in these geographic areas. In the generally wetter, eastern riparian states, where water availability historically did not pose a problem to settlement and land development, water users share the water resources without the strict limits imposed by appropriation systems. The western states typically are drier and experience regular water shortages. The prior appropriation system allows water users to acquire well-defined rights to water as a limited resource that requires planning to avoid scarcity. Over time, these systems have been the subject of debate as to the most effective way to manage water resources to minimize shortages in both eastern and western states.

Issue

The Commission's examination of water law led to recommendations intended to account for the fact that water supply is limited and "should be deployed in such a fashion as to yield the highest return to social well-being."[113] The Commission's focus on the scarcity of water as a resource and the importance of adapting water usage and allocation to promote efficiency led to recommendations that were intended to improve the accountability of water uses. That is, the recommendations suggested that certain procedural mechanisms and legal regulations be implemented to ensure that water was being used efficiently or effectively.

NWC Recommendations

The Commission's water rights recommendations fell into three categories: (1) transfer of water rights under the appropriation doctrine; (2) recognition of social values in water; and (3) permit systems for riparian states.

Transfer of Water Rights under Appropriation Doctrine

The Commission's recommendations stemmed from its assertion that the reallocation of water rights from low-value users to high-value users "would increase the benefits gained from the use of water and would tend to delay or make unnecessary the construction of new sources of supply."[114] The Commission outlined several areas in which water laws might be improved to meet the goal of more efficient reallocation, including (1) improving states' water rights records; (2) simplifying transfer procedures; (3) modifying legal constraints and prohibitions on transfers of water rights; and (4) evaluating federal water supply projects. Improving water rights records and simplifying transfer procedures are matters left for the states under their authority to regulate water rights, and no federal action would be taken to implement the recommendations with regard to those categories. However, the Commission's recommendations regarding legal reforms on transfers and supply projects was directed in part at federal activity.

The Commission recommended "the repeal of laws that forbid transfer, and the clarification of laws that obscure the power of water rights holders to make transfers."[115] According to the Commission's report, the law is unclear about the nature of the title that Reclamation holds to the water it supplies for irrigation use in the West.[116] Thus, the Commission recommended that Congress "remove the uncertainties and complexities in Federal ... law concerning title to water rights."[117] To achieve that end, one recommendation suggested that Congress declare a national policy that would permit and facilitate the transfer of water rights, particularly through the authorization of transfer of rights without the consent of the federal agency supplying the water so long as financial obligations have been repaid. The suggested federal action would allow blanket consent for transfers if the government had no financial claims against the users. In cases where financial obligations were not satisfied, the Commission recommended that the federal agency consent to water rights transfer so long as arrangements are made for payment to the United States either in lump sum or through assumption of contractual repayment obligations.

In its final recommendation for improvement of water supply management, the Commission recommended that Congress require every report for proposed water projects include a study detailing the supplies available to the area, the value of the water presently used in the area, the estimated value of the use to be supplied by the projects, and the feasibility of meeting demand for new supply by transferring rights from old uses to new uses. The Commission believed it would be "likely that construction of new water supply projects can be postponed in some areas for considerable lengths of time, that an economic incentive will be provided for saving water ... , that water will be put to better use as to maximize the economic yield to society, and that accordingly, the allocation of resources will be made more efficient."[118]

Recognition for Social Values of Water

The Commission recommendations were critical of the ability of both water rights systems, especially the appropriation system, to give "adequate recognition to social (that is, noneconomic) values in water."[119] Specifically, the Commission explained that the appropriation system developed under a preference "for economic development over protection of such social values as esthetics, recreation, and fish and wildlife propagation."[120] Although the Commission recognized that riparian systems allowed for greater protection of such values, it recommended that states using either system seek to improve the protection of these values.

The Commission noted two specific problems with the appropriation system, the lack of preservation of instream values and the inability of users to acquire rights for noneconomic purposes. Accordingly, it recommended that all states authorize water rights "for all social uses, noneconomic as well as economic."[121] It also recommended that states authorize and expand public water rights to protect streamflows, improve navigability, and prevent abuse. These recommendations were directed toward state governments, as states regulate water rights.

Permit Systems for Riparian States

The riparian system of water rights developed in areas where water scarcity was not a problem. However, over time, these areas have faced new climate conditions including drought and flooding, which have spurred debate over whether the riparian system can adequately deal with increased populations and decreased security of water resources. Critics of the riparian system argue that the system does not plan for water shortages and thus does not provide an efficient system of water resources management as a permit system does. The Commission's recommendations regarding modifications to the riparian system included a requirement for withdrawal permits in all cases, removal of restrictions on who could use water or where it must be located, issuance of temporal permits, and authorization for administrative agencies to act with consideration to social values in water use.

Current Status and Implementation

Because water supply and water rights issues are generally addressed and resolved at the state level, the transfer and permitting of water rights has not been implemented at the federal level. The federal government has taken more steps in recognizing social values in water.

Recognition for Social Values of Water

Although the Commission's recommendations were directed at state governments, Congress has enacted legislation over the last several decades that recognizes social values in decisions pertaining to waters regulated by federal water projects or otherwise under federal jurisdiction. The legislation has been both of general application and specifically targeted to certain federal water projects. The Wild and Scenic Rivers Act of 1968 (P.L. 90-542, 82 Stat. 906) allowed the federal government to ensure protection of certain waters from development.[122] Although the Wild and Scenic Rivers Act was enacted prior to the Commission's recommendations, Congress has continued to designate rivers for protection over the past four decades, in addition to those originally protected by the act. Designation under the act allows the federal government to recognize aesthetic and recreational values of the rivers and prevent uses that would diminish those values, principles reflected in the Commission's recommendations. In 1992, Congress enacted the CVPIA, which amended the original authorization for the Central Valley Project—a major federal water supply project in California—to include consideration of fish and wildlife preservation. The CVPIA also specifically allocated 800,000 acre-feet of project water for fish and wildlife purposes,[123] giving additional support to some of the goals highlighted by the Commission's recommendations.

Regarding Commission recommendations aimed at state law, many states have developed legal systems that recognize social values in the water resources of the state.[124] However, specific analysis of state actions following the Commission's report are beyond the scope of this analysis.

Modification of States' Appropriation and Riparian Water Rights Systems

The Commissions' recommendations regarding a federal role in water rights transfers in an appropriation system have not been implemented. While there has been limited action to encourage water transfers, no blanket national policy has been declared in accord with the Commission's recommendations. With respect to the commission's other federal recommendations regarding water supply management, the federal government has not implemented a uniform requirement for water use and supply reports on federal projects. This information may be gathered for other purposes under federal law, though.

A number of traditionally riparian states have modified their systems to account for permitting concerns.[125] The modified versions of the riparian system are generally referred to as regulated riparianism, and although these systems vary greatly by state, they generally include an administrative permitting requirement.[126] Because the law of water rights, including the specific system that a state uses, is a matter of state discretion, the federal government's action is limited by principles of federalism—general deference to the states, primacy in water allocation—and there has been no relevant federal action in modifying the riparian system according to the Commission's recommendations.

Indian Water Rights[127]

Issue

The Commission's chapter on Indian water rights framed the issue as a conflict in the West between Indians' rights to water and water development, on the one hand, and the potential harm to extensive non-Indian water development and use on the other.[128] The Commission described a situation in the West in which the water supply was limited and nearly all appropriated; Indian water rights claims were probably valid and were large but unquantified; Indian claims threatened to harm current non-Indians' water use and impede future water development; and the resultant uncertainties created an urgent need to resolve Indian water rights claims. Many perceive this as still being the case.[129] (For information on Indian reserved water rights, see CRS Report RL32198, *Indian Reserved Water Rights: An Overview*, by Yule Kim and Cynthia Brougher.)

NWC Recommendations

The Commission recommended general solutions for the entire West regarding Indian water rights, embodied in six official recommendations (some including multiple recommendations) for federal executive, congressional, and judicial actions. Chief among the recommendations were:

- that the executive branch should "define and quantify Indian water rights";[130]

- that Congress should pass legislation to "provide a substitute water supply or pay just compensation" to off-reservation owners of water rights harmed by Indian water resource projects; and
- that Congress should pass legislation placing "[j]urisdiction of all actions affecting Indian water rights" in federal courts, not state courts.[131]

Other Commission recommendations included:

- Interior Department quantification of existing water uses on Indian reservations;
- prior final adjudication of Indian water rights for federally assisted water projects, where the rights might impair water supplies, before authorization of the project;
- a law creating a standing federal offer to lease Indian tribes' water, at fair market rates, on all fully appropriated streams;
- federal initiation and funding of litigation to adjudicate tribes' water rights; and
- federal funding to assist tribes to develop their water.

Current Status and Implementation
While some Commission recommendations have been followed (at least in part), in general what has developed in the West are case-by-case settlements of specific Indian water rights claims, not broad solutions applied to all claims.

Quantification of Indian Water Rights
This Commission recommendation has been addressed, although perhaps not as completely as the Commission envisioned and not necessarily because of the Commission's recommendation. The Interior Department's Bureau of Indian Affairs (BIA) began inventorying and quantifying Indian water rights in 1971 (two years before the Commission's recommendations were announced), for purposes of contemporary and future litigation as well as reservation development.[132] Some tribes, and the two leading national Indian organizations, opposed BIA's quantification, fearing that "quantification may impose limits on the extent of their water rights entitlement, precluding future reservation water claims" and that a final quantification "is inconsistent with the openendedness of the right itself."[133] BIA continued quantifying water rights despite limited funding (although not if the tribe on a reservation

objected)[134] and BIA currently still assists tribes in technical studies, including quantification, for purposes of water rights negotiations and litigation.[135] Complicating the Commission's recommendation for executive quantification, however, are the facts that:

- the technological, economic, environmental, climatological, social, and evidentiary factors underlying a quantified amount may change over time;[136]
- BIA or tribal quantifications must compete with other parties' calculations; and
- a "final" quantification must be determined among all parties through negotiations, the judicial process (as the Commission recognized), or both.

Compensation to Off-Reservation Water Users

The Commission foresaw that Indian water resource development, based on confirmed Indian water rights, might well "take, destroy, or impair" off-reservation water users' rights to, and supply of water. In response, the Commission recommended that the United States "provide a substitute water supply or pay just compensation" to the off-reservation users (provided the off- reservation users did not know of the conflicting Indian water rights) at no cost to the Indian projects. Tribes, the BIA, and non-Indian water users opposed this recommendation, and it was never carried out. One commentator states that "Congress never even pretended to take [this and the other] recommendations seriously; none ever became law or even came close."[137] The BIA in 1973 considered the recommendation inequitable, because it created a legal protection for those who had ignored Indian water rights for years after the Supreme Court's 1908 Winters decision,[138] and because "it would make the development of projects for the use of water on Indian reservations economically impossible."[139] The National Tribal Chairmen's Association echoed these objections in 1974, testifying that "if the cost of 'buying off' junior appropriatees must be included in the total costs of an Indian water development project ..., such Indian development will be financially hopeless."[140]

Federal Jurisdiction in Indian Water Rights Litigation

The Commission's recommendation that the federal district courts should have sole "jurisdiction of all actions affecting Indian water rights" has not been implemented. Because of the U.S. Supreme Court's 1976 ruling in

Colorado River Water Conservation District v. United States,[141] federal courts no longer hear Indian water rights claims if there are concurrent state proceedings available. In that case, the Supreme Court determined that the primary policy goal of the McCarran Amendment,[142] which allowed federal reserved water rights claims to be addressed by state courts, was to designate state courts as the primary adjudicatory forums to resolve these issues. The Supreme Court concluded that providing a federal forum to address water rights claims would adversely affect the finality of the state proceedings since the two courts could contradict each other. Thus, the Supreme Court ruled that federal courts should defer to state courts by abstaining from these cases.

Other Recommendations

Among the other Commission recommendations, those for federal initiation and funding of litigation to adjudicate tribes' water rights, for federal funding to assist tribal water development, and for BIA quantification of existing Indian water uses were already being carried out and continue to be carried out.[143]

The Commission recommendation that federally assisted water projects be put on hold until relevant Indian water rights were adjudicated has not been implemented. Given the wide geographic distribution of Indian reservations and potential water rights claims in the West, it is likely that such a moratorium would affect a large number of federal, state, and private water projects, making its enactment into law problematic. On the other hand, federal assistance for water supply projects slowed considerably after publication of the Commission report in 1973.

The Commission recommendation involving leasing has also not been implemented. The Commission recommended that Congress enact legislation providing that, on fully appropriated streams to whose water Indians have a valid claim, the federal government make a standing offer to the Indian rights owners to lease their water or water rights at fair market value. Given the widespread and unquantified nature of Indian water rights, the costs of making this recommendation a federal policy would be difficult to calculate (and might be quite high).

CONCLUSION

While progress has been made on many of the problems identified by the Commission, few actions can be directly traced to the Commission's 1973 recommendations. Instead, it appears that water policy has continued to evolve—albeit in some areas, much as the Commission predicted— and that this evolution has had many underlying drivers, including but not limited to the findings of the Commission.

Many of the problems identified by the Commission remain today. Project planning has moved away from the recommended multi-objective or river basin planning approach recommended by the Commission. Water resource projects today are still largely authorized in piecemeal fashion, and water programs are rarely coordinated. Shifts in organizations and institutional arrangements since 1973 have reduced coordination of federal water agencies and planning. Available funding and political clout in some cases appear to be the significant factors in successfully pursuing projects, instead of overall benefits to the nation. State-federal tensions over proper and respective roles and responsibilities in water resource development, management, and allocation, continue to cloud resolution to the most difficult water resource issues.

Expectations for a commission to directly achieve changes in a system resistant to transformation may be unreasonable. Instead the influence of a commission may be how its recommendations combine with other drivers to create sufficient support for an evolution in policy.

APPENDIX: FUNDAMENTALS OF THE NATIONAL ENVIRONMENTAL POLICY ACT (NEPA)[144]

Signed into law on January 1, 1970, the National Environmental Policy Act (NEPA; P.L. 91-190, 42 U.S.C. §4321 et seq.) declared a national policy to protect the environment. To implement this policy, NEPA requires federal agencies to provide a detailed statement of environmental impacts, subsequently referred to as an environmental impact statement (EIS), for every recommendation or report on proposals for legislation and other major federal action *significantly* affecting the quality of the human environment. Although NEPA also created the Council on Environmental Quality (CEQ) in the

Executive Office of the President, it did not authorize CEQ to promulgate regulations to implement the EIS requirement or to enforce the law.

NEPA establishes the basic framework for integrating environmental considerations into federal decision making. However, the law itself does not detail how this process should be accomplished. With an initial absence of regulations specifying implementation procedures, and no agency authorized to enforce its requirements, federal agencies reacted in different ways to NEPA's requirements. In the 1970s, many agencies had difficulty complying with the law. In addition to the courts, CEQ played a significant role in determining how NEPA would be implemented although it had no enforcement authority. During the 1970s, CEQ issued non-binding guidelines for basic requirements of EIS preparation. CEQ left NEPA implementation largely to the federal agencies, which were to use the CEQ guidelines to prepare their own procedures.

During the early 1970s, there were frequent complaints regarding the delays that the NEPA process was perceived to cause. Some observers attributed these problems to a lack of uniformity in NEPA implementation and uncertainty regarding what was required of federal agencies. Also, in response to increasing NEPA-related litigation, agencies often produced overly lengthy, unreadable, and unused EISs. In an effort to standardize an increasingly complicated NEPA process, President Carter directed CEQ to issue regulations that would be legally binding on federal agencies;[145] final regulations became effective on July 30, 1979.[146] The CEQ regulations were intended to be generic in nature. Each federal agency was required to develop its own NEPA procedures that would be specific to typical classes of actions undertaken by that agency.[147] Separately, CEQ regulations directed federal agencies to review their existing policies, procedures, and regulations to ensure that they were in full compliance with the intent of NEPA.[148]

End Notes

[1] For example, the 110th Congress considered establishing a "Twenty-first Century Water Policy Commission" (H.R. 135 and S. 2728; see also Title VII of H.R. 2701). H.R. 135 has been reintroduced in the 111th Congress. Other legislation may also address water resource or wastewater management issues addressed by the 1973 NWC (e.g., the Secure Water Act (Title IX, Subtitle F, of P.L. 111-11) and water infrastructure legislation), but do not establish a commission similar to the NWC.

[2] NWC, *Water Policies for the Future: Final Report to the President and to the Congress of the United States* (Washington: GPO, 1973), 579 pp., hereafter referred to as the 1973 NWC Report.

[3] Due to this focus, little attention is given to the energy/water nexus, water resources research, supply augmentation, or technological and methodological changes in water resources management. Similarly, this CRS report focuses on federal or national policy and does not, except in limited circumstances, discuss recommendations aimed at state and local governments. This focus allows for greater attention to what has been accomplished, what problems remain unresolved, and what additional concerns have developed at the federal level.

[4] This is not generally a question of what powers the federal government has and could exercise under the Constitution. Rather, it is a recognition that Congress has often required that the United States defer to or comply with state law in the construction and operation of federal facilities pertaining to allocation, control, or distribution of water (see, for example, §8 of the Reclamation Act of 1902, 32 Stat. 390; 43 U.S.C. 372, 383). Other laws recognizing state primacy and their effects have been the subject of much judicial interpretation. At the same time, as owner of hundreds of thousands of acres of public domain land, the federal government is the "owner of the right to use the waters pertaining to the public domain lands, the right to use of which has not passed into private ownership under authority of the U.S. or an earlier sovereign." (Letter from Kent Frizzell, Assistant Attorney General, Land and Natural Resources Division, Department of Justice, to the National Water Commission, January 11, 1973.) The federal government also holds reserved water rights—although in many cases unquantified—for reservations of federal lands withdrawn from the public domain (e.g., national forests, national park lands, and wilderness areas). For example, see CRS Report RL30809, *The Wild and Scenic Rivers Act and Federal Water Rights*, by Cynthia Brougher.

[5] See, for example, *Water in the West: Challenge for the Next Century,* June 1998, Appendix C, Western Water Policy Review Advisory Commission. A minimum of 12 standing committees in the House and Senate have jurisdiction over various components of federal water policy; moreover, this figure excludes the extensive responsibilities of the appropriations committees in both chambers, and the direct and indirect activities of the budget, finance, and oversight committees in both houses.

[6] See, for example, the January 6, 2003, and February 20, 2007, letters from the American Water Resources Association (AWRA) to President George W. Bush et al., calling upon the Administration and Congress to develop a "national water vision" and policy to translate that vision into action. Available at http://awra.org/pdf/fnwpd.pdf; accessed February 12, 2009.

[7] These efforts included the Commission on Reorganization of the Executive Branch of the Government (First Hoover Commission, 1949); the President's Water Resources Policy Commission (Truman Administration, 1950); the Subcommittee to Study Civil Works, House Committee on Public Works (Jones Subcommittee, 1952); the Commission on Organization of the Executive Branch of the Government (Second Hoover Commission, 1955); the Commission on Intergovernmental Relations (1955); the Presidential Advisory Committee on Water Resources Policy (Eisenhower Administration, 1955); the Senate Select Committee on National Water Resources (1961); the Water Resources Council (1965-1983); the National Water Commission (1973); the National Commission on Water Quality (1976); the National Council on Public Works Improvement (1988); and the Western Water Policy Advisory Review Commission (1998). For more information on these efforts, see *Reorganization Efforts Affecting the Corps of Engineers Civil Works Mission*, by Martin Reuss, former historian for the U.S. Army Corps of Engineers, undated white paper; and U.S. House of Representatives, House Resources Committee, Water & Power Subcommittee, Hearings on the Twenty-first Century National Water Commission, testimony of Betsy A. Cody, May 22, 2002.

[8] According to Theodore M. Schad, former executive director of the NWC, "[results of the] Kerr Committee [Senate Select Committee on National Water Resources] had a much better reception and was essentially implemented within a few years which is unusual for a study

commission report. The key reason was that the study was made by people who were in a position to influence the implementation of the recommendations, which is a lot different from a presidential commission where the appointees are appointed and do their work and then are gone." Martin Reuss, Office of History and Institute for Water Resources, U.S. Army Corps of Engineers, *Water Resources People and Issues, Interview with Theodore M. Schad* (Alexandria, VA: U.S. Army Corps of Engineers, Jan. 1999), p. 166. Hereafter *Reuss Interview with Schad.*

[9] P.L. 90-515; 82 Stat. 868.

[10] Ibid.

[11] Theodore M. Schad, *The National Water Commission Revisited,* Water Resources Bulletin, American Water Resources Association, vol. 14, no.2, April 1978, p. 303. Hereafter *National Water Commission Revisited.*

[12] *Reuss Interview with Schad,* EP870-1-61, p. 166.

[13] The National Water Commission Act passed in September 1968, and the "nucleus" of the Commission staff of 19 was assembled by June 30, 1969. The maximum number of staff employed was 44 in June of 1971. The Commission met monthly from November 1968. President Nixon made changes to the Commission in 1969 and 1970. U.S. Congress, Senate Interior and Insular Affairs Committee, Subcommittee on Water and Power Resources, *National Water Commission Report,* hearings, June 28 and July 17, 1973, 93rd Cong., 1st sess. (Washington: GPO, 1973), p. 8.

[14] According to Theodore M. Schad, "The membership was very well balanced politically, geographically, and environmentally." *Reuss Interview with Schad,* pp. 168-169.

[15] *National Water Commission Revisited,* p. 305.

[16] Ibid.

[17] *National Water Commission Revisited,* p. 306. These seven themes also are articulated in Chairman Luce's testimony before the Senate Interior and Insular Affairs Committee (U.S. Congress, Senate Interior and Insular Affairs Committee, Subcommittee on Water and Power Resources, *National Water Commission Report,* hearings, June 28 and July 17, 1973, 93rd Cong., 1st sess. (Washington: GPO, 1973).)

[18] For several decades leading up to the 1960s, the federal government had played a large role in development of the nation's resources—largely through the construction of large dams and extensive projects, with little integrated planning.

[19] "Economic and Environmental Principles and Guidelines for Water and Related Land Resources Implementation Studies" (Principles and Guidelines), available at http://www.usace.army.mil/cw/hot_topics/ht_2008/pandg_rev.htm.

[20] §2031, Water Resources Development Act of 2007, P.L. 110-114 (42 U.S.C. § 1962-3).

[21] For an introduction to this ongoing struggle, see T. R. Reid, *Congressional Odyssey, the Saga of a Senate Bill* (New York: W. H. Freeman and Company, 1980).

[22] "Water Commission: No More Free Rides for Water Users," *Science,* April 13, 1973, p. 167.

[23] 1973 NWC Report, p. 2.

[24] Prepared by Nicole T. Carter, Specialist in Natural Resources Policy, Resources, Science, and Industry Division.

[25] Prior to development of planning "Principles and Standards" by the WRC in the late 1960s and early 1970s, project planning focused on project costs, benefits, and engineering feasibility.

[26] "Economic and Environmental Principles and Guidelines for Water and Related Land Resources Implementation Studies" (Principles and Guidelines), available at http://www.usace.army.mil/cw/hot_topics/ht_2008/pandg_rev.htm.

[27] §2031, Water Resources Development Act of 2007, P.L. 110-114 (42 U.S.C. § 1962-3).

[28] The 2008 Treasury-based rate for long-term yields was 4.875%; however, recent volatility in the U.S. financial system may result in very different projections of long-term yields.

[29] Western Water Policy Review Advisory Commission, *Water in the West: Challenge for the Next Century,* June, 1998, p. xvi.

[30] Ibid.

[31] Ibid., p. xxviii.

[32] April 3, 1998 letter from Representative Don Young and Senator Ted Stevens to Denise Fort, Chair of the Western Water Policy Review Advisory Commission, reprinted in Appendix B of the Commission's report, *Water in the West: Challenge for the Next Century,* June 1998.

[33] Prepared by Linda Luther, Analyst in Environmental Policy, Resources, Science, and Industry Division.

[34] In this context, environmental values appears to mean an interest or concern about the environmental impacts of a project.

[35] Commission recommendations addressed in this section include those associated with water resources projects likely to require a permit or some other authorization from the federal government and hence to be subject to NEPA. The Commission also included recommendations aimed at streamlining federal licensing procedures, particularly the licensing of hydroelectric facilities, including resolution of respective federal and state roles. Response to licensing recommendations is beyond the scope of this section and therefore not included in this discussion.

[36] Council on Environmental Quality, *Ninth Annual Report of the Council on Environmental Quality*, December 1978, pp. 396-399; and at 40 C.F.R. §§ 1500.4 and 1500.5.

[37] 40 C.F.R. § 1502.25.

[38] Prepared by Linda Luther, Analyst in Environmental Policy, Resources, Science, and Industry Division.

[39] 40 C.F.R. § 1500.2(d).

[40] 40 C.F.R. § 1506.6.

[41] In December 2007, CEQ released a citizen guide to help the public navigate the NEPA process, *A Citizen's Guide to the NEPA: Having Your Voice Heard*, available at http://ceq.hss.doe.gov/nepa/Citizens_Guide_Dec07.pdf.

[42] Prepared by Nicole T. Carter, Specialist in Environmental and Natural Resources Policy, Resources, Science, and Industry Division.

[43] Some smaller programs remain (e.g., USDA's NRCS small watershed program); however, none are on the scale of what was anticipated under the WRC and river basin commissions.

[44] National Research Council, National Academy of Sciences, *Confronting the Nation's Water Problems: The Role of Research* (Washington, DC: National Academies Press, 2004).

[45] Ibid.

[46] 1973 NWC Report, p. 389.

[47] Prepared by Nicole T. Carter, Specialist in Natural Resources Policy, Resources, Science, and Industry Division.

[48] Chapter 2 also discussed development and impacts of water projects in the Great Lakes; however, this topic is not reviewed in this report.

[49] Prepared by Pervaze A. Sheikh, Specialist in Environmental and Natural Resources Policy, and Nicole T. Carter, Specialist in Natural Resources Policy, Resources, Science, and Industry Division.

[50] The H. John Heinz Center for Science, Economics, and the Environment, *The State of the Nation's Ecosystems* (Cambridge University Press: Cambridge, England, 2002).

[51] U.S. Office of Science and Technology Policy, National Science and Technology Council, Subcommittee on Water Availability and Quality, the Committee on Environment and Natural Resources, *A Strategy for Federal Science and Technology to Support Water Availability and Quality in the United States* (Washington, DC: National Science and Technology Council, Sept. 2007).

[52] For more information on water quality activities, see the National Water Quality Assessment Program, available at http://water.usgs.gov/nawqa/.

[53] National Wetland Inventory, at http://www.nwi.fws.gov.

[54] Advisory Committee on Water Information, at http://acwi.gov/index.html.

[55] Ecosystem services include provisioning services such as food, water, timber, and fiber; regulating services which affect climate, floods, disease, wastes, and water quality; cultural

services which provide recreational, aesthetic, and spiritual benefits; and supporting services such as soil formation, photosynthesis, and nutrient cycling.

[56] Prepared by Nicole T. Carter, Specialist in Natural Resources Policy, Resources, Science, and Industry Division.

[57] For example, the Commission recommended ensuring full and equitable consideration of all practicable alternatives, higher beneficiary cost-sharing, and stronger local floodplain regulation, as well as eliminating windfall gains to private landowners.

[58] For example, see Interagency Floodplain Management Review Committee, *Sharing the Challenge: Floodplain Management into the 21st Century* (Washington, DC: Administration Floodplain Management Task Force, June 1994).

[59] A contribution of flood policy reports initiated by WRDA 2007 may be to clarify what is meant by "wise use" of floodplains and what kinds of restrictions wise use might entail.

[60] For more information on the NFIP and repetitive loss issues, see CRS Report RL32972, *Federal Flood Insurance: The Repetitive Loss Problem*, by Rawle O. King.

[61] American Institutes for Research, *The Evaluation of the National Flood Insurance Program Final Report* (Washington, DC: American Institutes for Research, Oct. 2006).

[62] For more information, see CRS Report RL33188, *Protecting New Orleans: From Hurricane Barriers to Floodwalls*, by Nicole T. Carter.

[63] Prepared by Harold Upton, Analyst in Natural Resources Policy, Resources, Science, and Industry Division.

[64] 1973 NWC Report, p. 31.

[65] For more analysis of planning, see this report's sections on "Water Resources Project Planning and Evaluation" and "Federal Water Resources Coordination."

[66] CZMA, P.L. 92-532; 16 U.S.C. 1451, et seq.

[67] P.L. 100-4; 16 U.S.C. 1330.

[68] U.S. Commission on Ocean Policy, "An Ocean Blueprint for the 21st Century," Final Report, September 2004, p. ES- 16.

[69] Office of the President, Council on Environmental Quality, *Conserving America's Wetlands 2008: Four Years of Progress Implementing the President's Goal*, April 2008.

[70] Prepared by Nicole T. Carter, Specialist in Natural Resources Policy, Resources, Science, and Industry Division.

[71] Prepared by Pervaze Sheikh and Harold Upton, Resources, Science, and Industry Division.

[72] 1973 NWC Report, p. 200.

[73] Ibid., p. 202.

[74] For more information on the Endangered Species Act, see CRS Report R40185, *The Endangered Species Act (ESA) in the 111th Congress: Conflicting Values and Difficult Choices*, by Eugene H. Buck et al.

[75] For example, the Pacific Northwest Electric Power Planning and Conservation Act (P.L. 96-501; 16 U.S.C. §839 note), affects certain operations of projects in the Columbia River Basin.

[76] See FWS, National Fish Habitat Action Plan website, available at http://www.fws.gov/fisheries

[77] Michael J. Bean and Melanie J. Rowland, *The Evolution of National Wildlife Law*, 3rd, ed., a project of the Environmental Defense Fund and World Wildlife Fund-U.S.(Westport, CT: Praeger, 1997), p. 416. Hereafter, *Evolution of National Wildlife Law*.

[78] *Evolution of National Wildlife Law*.

[79] See, for example, research provisions under the Pacific Northwest Electric Power Planning and Conservation Act (P.L. 96-501; 16 U.S.C. §839 note).

[80] All states have agencies working to conserve fish populations and provide opportunities for recreational fisheries. These efforts are conducted at the state level and regional level. For eastern coastal states, the states manage fisheries through multi-state associations (e.g., the Atlantic States Marine Fisheries Commission). The Gulf of Mexico and Pacific have similar regional bodies, but their priorities are focused on coordination and data collection. Also,

individual states protect fisheries resources through state endangered and threatened species programs, similar to the federal program.

[81] Payments to states were nearly $400 million for FY2008.

[82] Prepared by Betsy A. Cody, Specialist in Natural Resources Policy, Resources Science and Industry Division. For ease of discussion, user fees and cost-sharing are discussed simultaneously; some may argue they should be treated separately as they serve slightly different functions.

[83] Additionally, because of favorable terms (e.g., high federal cost-shares for federal flood control projects relative to water supply projects), some local sponsors have couched proposed projects as primarily flood control project to gain more federal funding. Similar approaches have been used in proposing "ecosystem restoration" or other environmental projects.

[84] 1973 NWC Report, p. 495.

[85] The report noted that an interagency committee had been established to avoid project sponsors "shopping" around for the most favorable federal assistance. It may have been referring to the WRC; several other chapters recommend using the WRC for coordination.

[86] 1973 NWC Report, p. 496.

[87] Congressional Quarterly Almanac, 99th Cong. 2nd sess. 1986, p. 109.

[88] Prepared by John Frittelli, Specialist in Transportation Policy, Resources, Science, and Industry Division.

[89] National Waterways Council, *The Origins and Development of the Waterways Policy of the United States,* Washington, D.C., 1967.

[90] 1973 NWC Report, pp. 120-121 and 497.

[91] The 10% cost recovery estimate is as per statement of John Paul Woodley, Jr., Assistant Secretary of the Army for Civil Works, at a press conference announcing the FY2008 USACE Civil Works Budget, Feb. 5, 2007.

[92] For example, the G. W. Bush Administration in 2008 proposed to phase out the existing barge fuel tax and replace it with a lockage fee system.

[93] For further legislative history of the 1978 act, see Senate Committee on Environment and Public Works, *A Legislative Background of the Waterway User Charges Legislation During the 95th Congress,* October 1978; and T. R. Reid, *Congressional Odyssey: The Saga of a Senate Bill* (San Francisco: W. H. Freeman, 1980).

[94] For further legislative history of the 1986 act, see Martin Reuss, former U.S. Army Corps of Engineers Historian, *Reshaping National Water Politics: The Emergence of the Water Resources Development Act of 1986,* October 1991.

[95] Federal Highway Administration, *Addendum to the 1997 Federal Highway Cost Allocation Study, Final Report,* May 2000.

[96] In addition to the study cited in footnote 94, others include CBO, *Paying for Highways, Airways, and Waterways: How Can Users Be Charged?* May 1992; CBO, *Inland Waterway Financing and the Potential Effects of User Charges,* Staff Working Paper, July 21, 1983; Leonard A. Shabman, *User Charges for Inland Waterways: A Review of Issues in Policy and Economic Impact,* May 1976; Charles River Associates, *A Study of the Inland Waterway Use Charge Program,* December 1970; American Enterprise Institute, *Waterway User Charges,* September 30, 1977.

[97] Prepared by Betsy A. Cody, Specialist in Natural Resources Policy, Resources Science and Industry Division.

[98] For example, in 1976, an organization of farmers and farmworkers known as National Land for People filed a lawsuit over sales of excess lands in the Westlands Water District in central California.

[99] In response to the National Land for People lawsuit, the Carter Administration undertook reviewed Reclamation land ownership both "westwide" (throughout the 17 reclamation states) and within the Westlands Water District, as part of an environmental impact statement on new rules and regulations regarding excess lands.

[100] April 3, 1998 letter from Representative Don Young and Senator Ted Stevens to Denise Fort, Chair of the Western Water Policy Review Advisory Commission, reprinted in Appendix B of the Commission's report, *Water in the West: Challenge for the Next Century*, June 1998.

[101] Prepared by Claudia Copeland, Specialist in Resources and Environmental Policy, Resources, Science, and Industry Division.

[102] Prepared by Claudia Copeland, Specialist in Resources and Environmental Policy, Resources, Science, and Industry Division.

[103] U.S. Environmental Protection Agency, "National Water Quality Inventory: Report to Congress, 2002 Reporting Cycle," EPA-841-R-07-001, October 2007, 39 p.

[104] For more information on the CWA, see CRS Report RL30030, *Clean Water Act: A Summary of the Law*, by Claudia Copeland.

[105] U.S. Congress, House of Representatives, Committee on Public Works and Transportation, *Final Report of the National Commission on Water Quality*, 94th Congress, 2d session, Mar. 22, 1976, H.Doc. 94-418.

[106] Performance standards specify particular technology-based treatment requirements, such as requiring all municipal sewage treatment plants to achieve secondary waste treatment, equivalent to about 85% removal of wastes.

[107] A water quality standard consists of the beneficial designated use or uses of a waterbody (e.g., recreation, or public water supply) and the water quality criteria (numeric or narrative) that are necessary to protect the designated uses.

[108] U.S. House of Representatives, Committee on Public Works and Transportation, "Federal Water Pollution Control Act Amendments of 1972," report together with additional and supplemental views to accompany H.R. 11896, 92nd Cong., 2nd sess., Report No. 92-911, p. 100.

[109] In the year before P.L. 92-500 was enacted, the total federal contribution was $1.25 billion, a level that took 10 years to reach. The 1972 legislation authorized a total of $18 billion over three years, beginning with $5 billion in FY1973.

[110] Prepared by Cynthia Brougher, Legislative Attorney, American Law Division.

[111] See generally, A. Dan Tarlock, Law of Water Rights and Resources, ch. 3 "Common Law of Riparian Rights."

[112] See generally, id. at ch. 5, "Prior Appropriation Doctrine."

[113] 1973 NWC Report, p. 260.

[114] Ibid., p. 260.

[115] Ibid., p. 264.

[116] Ibid., p. 264.

[117] Ibid., p. 270.

[118] Ibid., p. 270.

[119] Ibid., p. 271.

[120] Ibid., p. 271.

[121] Ibid., p. 278.

[122] See CRS Report RL30809, *The Wild and Scenic Rivers Act and Federal Water Rights*, by Cynthia Brougher.

[123] Section 3406(b)(2) of the CVPIA provides the 800,000 acre-feet of water for fish and wildlife purposes, and which is known as "b2 water."

[124] See, for example, CRS Report RL34554, *California Water Law and Related Legal Authority Affecting the Sacramento-San Joaquin Delta*, by Cynthia Brougher. California follows the public trust doctrine, the rule of reasonable use, and the no injury rule, all of which are intended to prevent misuse of water resources to the detriment of (continued...) other users' interests, whether economic or noneconomic, personal or statewide.

[125] See Joseph W. Dellapenna, Regulated Riparianism, in Waters and Water Rights § 9.01 (Robert E. Beck ed., LEXIS Repl. 2007: "Given the limitations of pure riparian rights as a system for allocating water among competing users during times of major water shortage, and the unworkability of importing prior appropriation law into the East, about half of the

eastern states have developed a new regulatory permit system based on riparian principles"
(citations omitted)).

[126] Ibid.

[127] Prepared by Roger Walke, Specialist in Indian Affairs Policy, Domestic Social Policy
Division, and Yule Kim, Legislative Attorney, American Law Division.

[128] 1973 NWC Report, p. 476. For more information on Indian water rights, see CRS Report
RL32198, *Indian Reserved Water Rights: An Overview*, by Yule Kim and Cynthia
Brougher.

[129] Western Governors' Association, *Water Needs and Strategies for a Sustainable Future*
(Denver: Western Governors' Association, 2006), p. 19.

[130] 1973 NWC Report, p. 477.

[131] Ibid., pp. 478-479.

[132] U.S. General Accounting Office, *Reserved Water Rights for Federal and Indian Reservations:
A Growing Controversy in Need of Resolution*, CED-78-176 (Washington: GAO, 1978), p.
21, hereafter referred to as *Reserved Water Rights*.

[133] *Reserved Water Rights*, p. 24.

[134] Daniel McCool, *Command of the Waters: Iron Triangles, Federal Water Development, and
Indian Water* (Tucson: University of Arizona Press, 1994), pp. 229-231, 242-244; *Reserved
Water Rights*, p. 24.

[135] U.S. Department of the Interior, *Indian Affairs: Budget Justification and Performance
Information, Fiscal Year 2009*, p. IA-RES-23.

[136] Rennard Strickland, ed., *Felix S. Cohen's Handbook of Federal Indian Law*, 1982 ed.
(Charlottesville, VA: Michie Bobbs-Merrill, 1982), p. 603, n. 29.

[137] Lloyd Burton, *American Indian Water Rights and the Limits of Law* (Lawrence: University
Press of Kansas, 1991), p. 129.

[138] *Winters* v. *United States*, 207 U.S. 564 (1908), found that when Congress set aside land for an
Indian reservation, it also impliedly reserved water rights for the reservation.

[139] "Comments of the Bureau of Indian Affairs on the National Water Commission Report," *in*
U.S. Congress, Senate Interior and Insular Affairs Committee, Subcommittee on Water and
Power Resources, *National Water Commission Report*, hearings, June 28 and July 17, 1973,
93rd Cong., 1st sess. (Washington: GPO, 1973), p. 394.

[140] U.S. Congress, Senate Interior and Insular Affairs Committee, Subcommittee on Indian
Affairs, *Indian Water Rights*, hearings, March 25-26, 1974, 93rd Cong., 2nd sess.
(Washington: GPO, 1974), p. 6.

[141] 424 U.S. 800 (1976).

[142] Act of July 10, 1952, 66 Stat. 549, 560 (codified at 43 U.S.C. § 666).

[143] *Command of the Waters*, pp. 112-160, 244; *Indian Affairs: Budget Justification*, FY2009, pp.
IA-TNR-20–IA-TNR22, IA-RES-22–IA-RES-24, and IA-CON-RM-1–IA-CON-RM-16.

[144] P.L. 91-190, 42 U.S.C. §4321 et seq.

[145] U.S. President (Carter), "Relating to Protection and Enhancement of Environmental Quality,"
Executive Order 11991, May 24, 1977, 42 *Federal Register* 26967.

[146] 43 *Federal Register* 55978, November 28, 1978; 40 C.F.R. §§ 1500-1508.

[147] 40 C.F.R. § 1507.3.

[148] 40 C.F.R. § 1500.6.

In: Water Policy Over 35 Years
Editors: Dillon J. Sykes

ISBN: 978-1-60876-754-0
© 2010 Nova Science Publishers, Inc.

Chapter 2

A STRATEGY FOR FEDERAL SCIENCE AND TECHNOLOGY TO SUPPORT WATER AVAILABILITY AND QUALITY IN THE UNITED STATES

National Science and Technology Council

INTRODUCTION

Water is essential to maintain human health, agriculture, industry, ecosystem integrity, and the economic vitality of communities and the Nation. Throughout history, a key measure of a civilization's success has been the degree to which human ingenuity has harnessed fresh water resources for the public good. Indeed, civilizations have failed because of their inability to provide a safe and reliable water supply in the face of changing water resources and needs.

U.S. Water Resources—Are We Facing a Shortage?

In its early history, U.S. water management focused largely on alleviating or controlling the impacts of floods and droughts. Investments in dams, water infrastructure, navigation infrastructure, canals, and water treatment plants provided safe, abundant, and inexpensive sources of water, aided flood management, and dramatically improved hygiene, health, and economic prosperity. The U.S. water resources, infrastructure, and technologies became the envy of the world.

Water-related science and technology have served our Nation well. The Nation has built infrastructure that provides safe drinking water, agricultural irrigation, hydropower, flood control, and navigable waterways. Through improved waste treatment technology, great strides have been made in improving water quality, and in protecting and enhancing habitat for aquatic organisms and recreational opportunities for the public.

The dawning of the 21st century brings a new set of water resource challenges. Climate variability and change, mining of finite ground water[1] resources, and degraded water quality dramatically impact the amount of fresh water available at any given time. The increasing competition among water users means that critical decisions will be made about allocating water for agricultural use and consumption by cities, for maintaining water reservoirs and ensuring in-stream flows for aquatic ecosystems, and for industrial and energy production and recreational uses. Even small changes in water quality, quantity, or the time when water resources are available can render water supplies useless for their intended applications or hazardous to life and property. Today, water quantity and water quality are equally critical to the long-term sustainability of the Nation's communities and ecosystems.

Authority to manage water resources is largely delegated to States, Tribes, and local municipalities. SWAQ is committed to productive collaboration with these water resource managers. SWAQ has identified a Federal role that emphasizes the variety of ways that water science and technology can be used to inform policies and decisions for managing water resources for the public good. As we, the citizens of the United States and governmental agencies at all levels, face today's national water resource challenges, the Nation will again rely on opportunities and tools offered by science and technology. Federal water research and development will increase the range of options and will inform the public, water managers, policymakers, and the private sector about the benefits, costs, and risks of the variety of decisions they face.

WHAT IS OUR CURRENT WATER USE?

Water use is usually defined and measured in terms of withdrawal and consumption—that which is taken and that which is used up. Withdrawal refers to water extracted from surface or ground water sources. Consumption is that part of a withdrawal that is ultimately used and removed from the immediate water environment by evaporation, transpiration, incorporation into crops or a product, or other consumption. Conversely, return flow is the portion of a withdrawal that is not consumed, but is instead returned to a surface or ground water source from a point of use and becomes again available for use. Returned water may be of impaired quality. For example, most of the water withdrawn for once-through cooling of thermoelectric power generation is returned as heated water to the surface water body. A fraction of the returned water evaporates, and the rest is available for other uses—perhaps, after reaching ambient temperature, thermoelectric cooling further downstream.

Current figures on water use in the United States are based on a mixture of measurements and estimates. Total water use is a combination of (1) in-stream use for hydropower generation, (2) withdrawals from surface and ground water sources for off-stream use, (3) in-stream use to support ecological needs, and (4) use of rainwater before it reaches a river or aquifer. We have estimates for (1) and (2). In 1995 in-stream use for hydropower was about 3,160,000 million gallons per day. This is about 2.6 times the average runoff of the United States, and reflects the fact that the same water is used to power multiple turbines as it flows through a series of dams. For total offstream water withdrawals (2), our best guess for 2000 is that these averaged 408,000 million gallons per day (Hutson and others, 2004). This is three times the average flow over Niagara Falls, or enough water to fill the Houston Astrodome every two minutes. Eighty-five percent of the water we withdraw is fresh; the rest is brackish or salty. Surface water provides 79 percent and ground water accounts for 21 percent. Since 1980, reductions in thermoelectric-power, irrigation, and industrial water use have helped to stabilize overall water withdrawals despite continued population growth. On the basis of estimates from 1995, the last year for which consumptive use was systematically estimated nationwide, about 30 percent of the fresh water withdrawals were used consumptively, and the remaining 70 percent were returned to surface-water bodies (Solly and others, 1998).

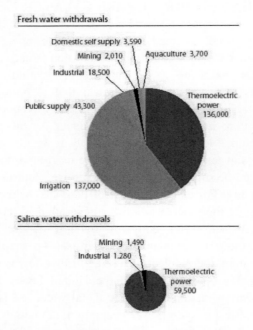

Total U.S. water withdrawals, 2000 (in million gallons per day)

Hutson, S.S., Barber, N.L., Kenny, J.F., Linsey, K.S., Lumia, D.S., and Maupin, M.A., 2004, Estimated use of water in the United States in 2000: U.S. Geological Survey Circular 1268, 46 p.
Solly, W.B., Pierce, R.R., and Perlman, H.A., 1998, Estimated use of water in the United States in 1995: USGS Circular 1200, 71p.

SCIENCE INFORMS WATER POLICY AND MANAGEMENT DECISIONS

Individuals, businesses, and government bodies make decisions daily about water use based on the physical, chemical, and biological properties of the water, as well as on economic, social, legal, and political considerations: Is there enough water? Is it clean enough to drink? Is the supply declining? How will climate variability and change affect future water availability? Can current water use be sustained? (See textbox, "What is our current water use?")

Scientists and engineers work to understand and quantify the complex factors that control water supply in order to strengthen water management decisions and provide new options. Scientific concepts and technological tools are used to measure the water supply, expand choices for water use, and reduce the uncertainties in water availability and quality. New measurement techniques, innovative observational network design, improved means for data access, and improved water-supply forecasting systems will help. Predictions of water availability over time are critical for decisionmakers, and are most useful when accompanied by estimates of their reliability. New technologies are being developed for pollution mitigation, water recovery and reuse, efficient water delivery systems, and crop management. Advances in biotechnology and nanotechnology and creative uses of low-quality water increase water management options.

New homes replace farmland in Iowa.

New frameworks for conceptualizing and handling the complexity of water availability, quality, and management issues consider interactions between various physical, chemical, biological, and social components; a systems approach to water management considers the multiple dimensions of competing demands. Effectively dealing with multiple competing demands requires quantitative methods to compare options and assess the tradeoffs among them. With adequate tools to model these complex systems, decision-makers will be able to assess consequences of specific policies and decisions under a broad range of scenarios. This will help the Nation use existing infrastructure more effectively and focus on expansion of the engineered and natural infrastructure where it is most needed.

French Broad River at Asheville, North Carolina. Long-term hydrologic records are used to establish flow status and trends. The USGS has measured streamflow at this site from 1895 to present; current real-time measurements are made in cooperation with the Tennessee Valley Authority.

PRINCIPLES FOR APPLYING SCIENCE AND TECHNOLOGY TO WATER AVAILABILITY AND QUALITY

Several previous reports have considered the research needs related to water resources and the requirements to make the science and technology most useful and effective (National Research Council, 1997, 2001, 2002, and 2004b; National Science and Technology Council, 2004; U.S. General Accounting Office, 2003, 2004). Important principles have emerged from these reports to guide the development of the science and technology needed to support water availability and quality:

- U.S. economic health and prosperity rely on adequate supplies of clean fresh water, and science and technology are fundamental to sustaining U.S. water supply.
- Advances in water science and technology should be applied at Federal, State, and local levels, should inform and be informed by private sector developments, and should be used to provide safe, reliable water supplies.
- "Water availability" has traditionally referred to the quantity of water. By consistently referring to "water availability and quality," we hope to further the idea that "available water" is a function of both water quantity and water quality. That is to say, poor water quality can render water unavailable for many uses.
- A key role for science and technology is to expand options for management and use of the Nation's water resources.
- Water users, managers, and scientists must work together to guide and develop the science and technology needed to support water availability and quality.
- Scientists and managers must employ a systems approach to fresh water withdrawals, use, and disposal that considers physical, chemical, biological, social, behavioral, and cultural aspects.
- Water law, economic incentives, public awareness, public education, and sensitivity to differences in value systems are cornerstones of effective water resource management.

SETTING A RESPONSIVE AND EFFECTIVE NATIONAL WATER-RESOURCES RESEARCH AGENDA [MODIFIED FROM NATIONAL RESEARCH COUNCIL, 2004B]

The business of setting priorities for water resources research needs to be more than a matter of summing up the priorities of the numerous Federal agencies, professional associations, and Federal committees. A rigorous process for priority setting should be adopted—one that will allow the water-resources research enterprise to remain flexible and adaptable to changing conditions and emerging problems. Such a mechanism is also essential to ensure that water-resources research needs are considered from a national and long-term perspective. The components of such a priority-setting process are outlined below, in the form of six questions or criteria that can be used to assess individual research areas and thus to assemble a responsive and effective national research agenda.

1. **Is there a Federal role in this research area?** This question is important for evaluating the "public good" nature of the water-resources research area. A Federal role is appropriate in those research areas where the benefits of such research are widely dispersed and do not accrue only to those who fund the research. Furthermore, it is important to consider whether the research area is being or even can be addressed by institutions other than the Federal government.

2. **What is the expected value of the research?** This question addresses the importance attached to successful results of direct problem-solving or advancement of fundamental knowledge of water resources.

3. **To what extent is the research of national significance?** National significance is greatest for research areas that address issues of large-scale concern, are driven by Federal legislation and mandates, and whose benefits accrue to a large swath of the public.

4. **Does the research fill a gap in knowledge?** Because of the complex nature of future water resources research, such research is likely to be interdisciplinary, have a broad systems context, incorporate uncertainty, and address the role of human and ecological adaptation to

changing water resources. Gaps in our understanding of these complex interactions are important to fill.

5. **How well is this research area progressing?** Past efforts should be evaluated with respect to funding levels and trends, whether the research area is a part of the agenda of one or more Federal agencies, and whether prior investments have produced results.

6. **How does the research area complement the overall water-resources research portfolio?** The portfolio approach is built on the premise that a diverse mix of holdings is the least risky way to maximize return on investments. The water-resources research agenda should be balanced in terms of the time scale of the effort (short-term vs. long-term), the source of the problem statements (investigator-driven vs. problem-driven), the goal of the research (fundamental vs. applied), and the investigators conducting the work (internally vs. externally conducted).

THE CHALLENGES OF MEETING FUTURE U.S. DEMANDS FOR WATER

In 1800, the 5.3 million citizens of the United States enjoyed virtually unlimited supplies of clean fresh water. When the geographic growth of the Nation ended in 1959, the United States had a population of 179 million. In 2006, the Nation supported 300 million citizens and the population was growing at a rate of almost 1 percent per year. Several regions and major metropolitan areas are growing at double-digit rates. Attempts to address the science and technology needs of the water community will require special consideration of areas with extreme growth in population or water consumption. In addition, trends in water use in the agricultural and energy sectors are major drivers of water resource needs. Other primary factors that influence the future availability of water include climate change and variability, pollution, and increased conflicts over water allocation among different users. Abundant supplies of clean, fresh water can no longer be taken for granted.

SCIENTIFIC AND TECHNICAL CHALLENGES TO ENSURE ADEQUATE WATER SUPPLY FOR THE NATION

Challenge 1

Measure and account for its water

Challenge 2

Develop methods that will allow expansion of fresh water supplies while using existing supplies more efficiently

Challenge 3

Develop and improve predictive water management tools

Authority for water resource management is generally delegated to States, Tribes, and localities. But water is crucial to the Nation's economic, social, and environmental conditions, and decisions in any given locality can have impacts far beyond their political boundaries. Given the importance of sound water management to the Nation's well-being, it is appropriate for the Federal government to play a significant role in providing information to all on the status of water resources and to provide the needed research and technology that can be used by all to make informed water management decisions. Decision-makers need three things to support sound management decisions: knowledge of current conditions; socially and technically feasible options that expand our water resources through efficiencies in use or treatments; and the means to evaluate the likely short- and long-term outcomes of their decisions. Water-resource choices belong to cities, States, Tribes, farmers, businesses, and individual citizens. The Federal role described in this report is to create the knowledge, the range of options, and the ability to predict outcomes so that those decisions can be as sound as possible.

The NSTC Subcommittee on Water Availability and Quality (SWAQ) sees three broad categories of scientific and technical challenges that the Nation must meet in order to ensure an adequate water supply:

Challenge 1

The United States should measure and account for its water

The United States should accurately assess the quantity and quality of its water resources, should accurately measure how water is used, and should know how water supply and use change over time

- Know water resources and how they are changing
- Many effective programs are underway to measure aspects of our water resources. However, simply stated, quantitative knowledge of U.S. water supply is currently inadequate (U.S. Government Accountability Office, 2005; National Research Council, 2004a). The United States should measure water resources more strategically and efficiently. A robust process for measuring the quantity and quality of the Nation's water resources requires a systems approach. Surface water, ground water, rainfall, and snowpack all represent quantities of water to be assessed and managed—from the perspectives of quantity, quality, timing, and location. A comprehensive assessment of U.S. water resources should build upon significant monitoring programs by water management authorities, States, and Federal government agencies to ensure that regional and national water resources are measured accurately. Data and information about the Nation's water supply should be widely available, should integrate physical and social sciences, and should be relevant to decisionmakers, from the individual homeowner to regional water managers. Without an adequate assessment of water supplies on a watershed or aquifer basis, optimal water management cannot be achieved. Improved knowledge of the size and distribution of the water supply and how it changes over time will allow more efficient and equitable allocation of this precious resource and will minimize overallocation of limited supplies.

NEW TECHNIQUES FOR MEASURING SEDIMENT

Suspended solids and sediments transport nutrients and other organic matter that are critical to the health of a water body. In natural quantities, suspended sediment replenishes streambed materials and creates valuable habitats such as pools and sand bars. But sediments and sediment-associated contaminants can also degrade the quality of receiving waters and damage the downstream ecosystem. In fact, excessive sediment is the leading cause of impairment of the Nation's surface waters (U.S. Environmental Protection Agency, 2000).

In most streams, the majority of suspended sediments are transported during high-flow periods, the very time when traditionally the fewest data were collected. New sediment-surrogate technologies—devices that infer properties of river sediments using partially or wholly automated methods—show considerable promise toward providing the types and density of river-sediment data needed for safer, quantifiably accurate, and cost-effective monitoring. In several projects across the Nation, the U.S. Geological Survey is cooperating with U.S. Bureau of Reclamation, U.S. Army Corps of Engineers, U.S. Environmental Protection Agency, U.S. Fish and Wildlife Service, State agencies in Virginia, Kansas, California, and Georgia, and university researchers to test instruments operating on bulk and digital optic, laser, pressure-difference, and acoustic technologies in riverine and laboratory settings for measuring fluxes and size characteristics of suspended sediment and bed-load, and for selected characteristics of bed material.

Although it is doubtful that any one technology will suffice for all of the Nation's sediment-monitoring needs, multifrequency hydroacoustics holds the most promise as a robust technique for wide-scale suspended-sediment monitoring. The potential exists to provide an unprecedented temporal data density—compared to historical measurements, for which daily data were once the norm—with minimal physical intrusion into the water column. To make the transition from research to operational applications, these new technologies must be rigorously tested with respect to accuracy and reliability in different physiographic settings, and their performances must be compared to those of traditional techniques. These new, more cost-effective technologies are crucial to diagnosing impairments of water bodies from sedimentation and to developing and confirming effective strategies for improvements in these conditions.

Controlled flow studies in the Colorado River

The Glen Canyon Dam cut off 94 percent of the sand formerly supplied to the Colorado River at the upstream boundary of Grand Canyon

National Park, and the amount of sand stored along the river has decreased by 25 percent over the past 20 years. The decreased size and abundance of sand bars in the Grand Canyon are indicators of the degree to which the post-dam ecosystem has been altered from the pre-dam condition. Results of controlled-flow studies indicate that an effective means of increasing sand bars is to immediately follow large tributary floods with artificial floods released from the dam. Laser-diffraction and acoustic technologies are now being used to monitor suspended-sediment transport in the Colorado River in Grand Canyon.

- Know water use
- To manage water effectively, we should know our present and future demands for water in individual homes, businesses, farms, industries, and power plants, as well as water needed for sustainable ecosystems. Furthermore, data and information about the Nation's demand for water should integrate physical and social sciences, should be widely available, and should be presented in a manner relevant to decisionmakers ranging from individual homeowners to regional water managers.
- Water-use studies should encompass combined surface-water and ground-water management. Water-use data should have seasonal resolution, and should be collected using a combination of measurement and statistical estimation.

Thermoelectric cooling towers

Compared to the usual flow and sediment content of the Colorado River (top), the river more than 2 hours and 30 km downstream from a tributary flood (bottom) has its streamflow increased by less than 3 percent, but the silt and clay content is increased 300–400 times and sand content increased 10–20 times (Rubin and others, 2002; Topping and others, 2005; Wright and others, 2005). Discovery of this type of discharge-independent change in sediment transport was made possible through the use of new sediment monitoring technologies.

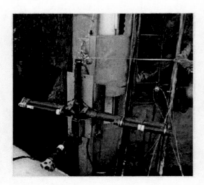

Three-frequency array of sideways-looking acoustic-Doppler current profilers deployed at the Grand Canyon streamgage

U.S. Environmental Protection Agency, Office of Water, 2002, National water quality inventory; 2000 Report (EPA- 841-R-02-001) accessed online 09/18/2006 at http://www. epa.gov/305b/2000report/

U.S. Environmental Protection Agency, Office of Water and Office of Science and Technology, August 2003, Developing water quality criteria for suspended and bedded sediments; potential approaches: 58 p.

Rubin, D.M., Topping, D.J., Schmidt, J.C., Hazel, J., Kaplinski, K., and Melis, T.S., 2002, Recent sediment studies refute Glen Canyon Dam hypothesis: EOS, American Geophysical Union Transactions, v. 83, n. 25, p. 273, 277-278.

Topping, D.J., Rubin, D.M., and Schmidt, J.C., 2005, Regulation of sand transport in the Colorado River by changes in the surface grain size of eddy sandbars over multiyear timescales: Sedimentology, v. 52, no. 5, p. 1133-1153.

Wright, S.A., Melis, T.S., Topping, D.J., and Rubin, D.M., 2005, Influence of Glen Canyon Dam operations on downstream sand resources of the Colorado River in Grand Canyon, in Gloss, S.P., Lovich, J.E., and Melis, T.S., eds., The state of the Colorado River ecosystem in Grand Canyon: U.S. Geological Survey Circular 1282, p. 17-3 1.

- **Know the role of ecosystems in maintaining water availability and quality**

   Society depends on important services provided by healthy aquatic and riparian ecosystems, such as water purification, provision of plant and animal foods, nonstructural flood control, recreation, nutrient cycling, and maintenance of biodiversity. In addition, aquifers, streams, wetlands, and riparian systems make up the natural water infrastructure, and the timing, quality, and volume of water available for human uses depends, in part, on ecosystems filtering, cleaning, and storing water. In the past, water resource management focused on meeting society's needs for water, with scant attention to water required to maintain healthy ecosystems. The unintended result is that ecosystem services have been compromised in many areas, often leading to costly restoration and exacerbating conflicts over water use. Increasingly, water managers are required to provide ecosystems with water needed to function and stay healthy. We should improve our ability to manage water resources in ways that reduce conflicts while maintaining the integrity of these ecosystems and the services they provide. We should evaluate the services provided by ecosystems, and assess how ecosystems complement and support the services provided by engineered infrastructure. A better understanding of the impact of engineered infrastructure on ecosystem resiliency and productivity will improve watershed management decisions.

- **Know the water infrastructure**

   The United States has invested enormous resources in the development and maintenance of water infrastructure—built infrastructure that is necessary for the Nation's continued health and economic well-being. Water infrastructure, much of it aging and constructed in a time of less competition for water, should be assessed regarding its condition and suitability to meet the Nation's water needs now and in the future. Treatment and delivery infrastructure is vital to communities, and the condition of levees, dams, navigation channels, and ports is also critical to U.S. water supplies. Decisionmakers need to know the vulnerabilities of water infrastructure to natural or manmade disasters.

   Recognizing this need, various inventories of infrastructure are maintained by various organizations. The need and opportunities to improve these infrastructure inventories should be explored to ensure that the water managers know when structures exceed their design lifespan, if structures are being properly maintained, if we can improve the operation of structures to better meet current water needs, and if we have adequately assessed flood risk. Water managers need information not only about the water itself, but about the built infrastructure that enables its beneficial use.

A researcher sets up a drip irrigation system for lettuce at an experimental station in Alaska.

Challenge 2

The United States should develop methods that will allow expansion of fresh water supplies while using existing supplies more efficiently

The United States possesses significant volumes of water that cannot currently be used because they are of marginal quality. The National water supply will be bolstered by the treatment and use of these marginal or impaired waters. Just as water managers now rely on information provided by scientists to make informed decisions about the use of existing water resources, so science and technology will help expand management choices and help expand the water supply. Expanding the water supply should be accomplished through technological means by making poor-quality water usable. Efficiency also plays an essential role; increased water efficiencies will be achieved through both technological and institutional mechanisms.

- **Develop tools to make more efficient use of existing water supplies and infrastructure**
  Energy efficiency is widely recognized as an economical means of reducing the need for new supplies of energy. The same is true for water. Thus, we should develop technologies for more efficient use of water in energy production, buildings, agriculture, industry, and for other demands. This will reduce the need for expanding sources of fresh water. Energy production and agriculture are the two sectors with highest demand for fresh water in the United States. New materials and designs will make electricity generation more efficient, producing more energy for every drop of water. New cooling technologies will sharply reduce water requirements for existing and state-of-the-art power plants. New agricultural technologies will yield more water-efficient and drought-resistant crops, generating more food for each volume of water. New technologies will reduce wastewater volumes in municipal and industrial processes. Science and technology will improve water delivery in canals, reduce leaks from pipes, and help control water-consuming weeds, thereby extending the lifespan of existing infrastructure. Finally, economists and social scientists may identify ways to improve acceptance or implementation of innovations in water use and water markets that will facilitate more efficient use of the existing supply.

- **Develop tools to expand water resources**

  The potential for science and technology to expand the fresh-water supply cuts across disciplines, scales, and topics. We should expand U.S. water resources by developing new treatment technologies, by preventing water pollution through better land-use practices, by adopting new approaches to storage, and by creating behavioral, social and economic tools that optimize spending and encourage acceptance of new water management techniques. Water that is currently unusable should be rendered usable with treatment technologies. Advanced water treatment technologies have become more economical, and removing the salt from saline or brackish waters provides a new source of fresh water for industry, agriculture, or communities. Scientific advances will allow us to improve advanced water treatment technologies to treat impaired waters for various uses and allow us to substitute low-quality or reused water for various purposes while at the same time protecting human and ecological health. Improved technologies should also enable better cleanup of waters from industry, energy production (coal, oil, and gas) and mining, or other technologies before the water is released back into the environment. Advanced technologies will also allow use of impaired water in lieu of fresh water for cooling and other thermoelectric generation needs.

Begonia bulbs are produced using reclaimed water.

Preventing water pollution by managing land-use practices may prove to be more cost-effective than treating contaminated water. In addition to improving the methods for treating impaired waters to make them suitable for use, we should develop and test land-use practices that help prevent the impairment of water and that enhance supplies within the watershed.

Storage and recovery of water should also be improved so that water not immediately needed for in-stream use may be saved for future use. Reliability of water supplies is enhanced by storing water from wet seasons or wet years for use in dry seasons or dry years. Aquifer storage and recovery is becoming more common. Hydrologic science should be used to answer questions about the feasibility and efficiency of aquifer storage; social sciences are needed to address issues of property rights and incentives.

Using behavioral and management sciences, we should develop a "toolbox" of public awareness and education, technology transfer, incentives, legal, institutional, and economic systems that affect water use to gain acceptance for water-saving technologies, water reuse, and markets for water quantity and quality. With these tools, managers will be able to develop strategies to increase adoption of water-saving technologies in agriculture, individual homes, and industry. We should apply behavioral and management sciences to reduce conflict and better manage competing demands on our water resources, and to develop ways to better incorporate scientific and technical information into water-resource decision-making. Social sciences will help managers make tradeoffs and manage risks to optimize agricultural yields, power production, municipal supplies, ecosystem viability, navigation reliability, and flood protection.

Challenge 3

The United States should develop and improve predictive water management tools

Today's decisions and policies will shape our water future. The effectiveness of those decisions depends on the quality of information and on incorporating knowledge about the reliability (or conversely, the uncertainty) associated with predictive management tools. In addition to improved water data, the United States should develop and expand a variety of forecasting and predictive models and systems. Scientists should improve our knowledge of how water resources change because of natural events and human actions. We should develop an array of tools, using behavioral, management, and other social sciences, to educate and influence water-use behavior of individual water users, businesses, industries, and resource managers.

- **Develop tools to anticipate the outcomes of short-term decisions about water release, withdrawal, storage, and use**

  Short-term predictive models or forecasting tools on time scales of hours to seasons are crucial to effective management of our water resources and water-resource infrastructure, and to the protection of public health and aquatic life. Predictions and forecasts support decisions such as to store or release water, divert water for off-stream use, treat water, or, in times of flood or water-quality incidents, keep the public and water users out of harm's way.

  These decisions are made while facing uncertainty about predictions. If that uncertainty is reduced and accurately described, then decisions will be made that tend to make for better use of the resource and increase public benefits and/ or reduce risk. There are many examples of situations where predictions incorrectly indicated that the upcoming season would be one of severe supply shortfalls. Based on incorrect predictions, managers instituted shortfalls of deliveries to users, resulting in severe, unnecessary negative consequences for water users. Alternatively, there are many examples where predictions incorrectly indicated supply abundance, yet shortfalls ensued. Improved forecasts will prevent costly mistakes and stretch the utility of existing supplies and infrastructure.

  Forecasts should be developed collaboratively among Federal agencies, local and State governments, the private sector, and universities and other educational institutions, as appropriate. Using data collected at appropriate scales and intervals, effective models will allow water managers to visualize hydrodynamics in real time and to anticipate the consequences of their management decisions.

- **Develop tools to anticipate the outcomes of long-term planning and policy decisions**

  Communities of water users and water resource managers should anticipate long-term water availability and quality on time scales of years to decades. They should base resource-management, planning, and policy decisions both on historical data and on predictions about future hydrologic, meteorologic, and ecologic conditions. For example, stakeholders should know that climate change is predicted to result in altered regional precipitation frequency and water resources (dryer conditions in some locations, wetter conditions in others). Both probabilistic and physical models for predicting long-term hydrologic, meteorologic, and ecologic conditions should provide the scientific basis for planning and policymaking. The very practical matter of communicating scientific information and modeling capabilities to decisionmakers and stakeholders is also important as we expand the use of predictive water management tools.

  Long-term planning and policy decisions—such as whether to build a dam, remove a dam, build a treatment plant or aquifer storage and recovery facility, install best management practices, change the laws, permit withdrawals, or change prices—are informed by predictions. Long-term models and other analyses should anticipate the effect of specific management decisions on water supply and quality and should be used to evaluate a range of water-policy options in advance of their implementation. Models and other analyses are useful for solving the types of conflicts over water resources that in the past have assumed a single "right" level of human use or ecological condition. By explicitly simulating ranges of human uses and achievable ecological conditions, effective models will provide a basis for predicting the future capacity of watersheds and aquifers to provide water supplies under a variety of scenarios, and they will thus provide a basis for management and policy decisions.

A breached levee along the Sacramento River, California, is being repaired.

Native grasses and trees in a conservation buffer along Bear Creek, Iowa.

A FEDERAL SCIENCE STRATEGY TO MEET U.S. WATER CHALLENGES

This report proposes a science and technology strategy to address the water challenges that face the United States. The current strategy builds on the earlier report of this Subcommittee (National Science and Technology Council, 2004). Each of the following seven strategic elements is intended to address one or more of the broad water challenges facing the Nation. The elements of Federal collaboration to implement the strategic plan are:

- Implement a National Water Census
- Develop a new generation of water monitoring techniques
- Develop and expand technologies for enhancing reliable water supply
- Develop innovative water-use technologies and tools to enhance public acceptance of them
- Develop collaborative tools and processes for U.S. water solutions
- Improve understanding of the water-related ecosystem services and ecosystem needs for water
- Improve hydrologic prediction models and their applications

Implement a National Water Census

Just as it is critical to the Nation to have up-to-date statistics on population, economic activity, agriculture, energy, and public health, it is also critical to know the status of our water resources. The United States has a strong need for an ongoing census of water that describes the status of our Nation's water resource at any point in time and identifies trends over time. The system will include all components of the natural and human water cycle: precipitation, snow pack, soil moisture, ground-water recharge and storage, river flow, reservoir storage, evaporation, water use, and infrastructure. Much data is already collected for these parameters, and agencies have already made a start at unifying this effort, but more complete information is needed so that policymakers and the public can ask simple questions such as: How much water do we have in this state or river basin today and how does that compare to a few months ago or a few decades ago? How is water use changing over time? What is the status of our engineered water infrastructure? What is the status of our ecosystem or natural water infrastructure? Answers to these questions should be easily accessible and in a form useful to water managers and the public. A National Water Census will require a combination of improvements in monitoring networks and sensors, software to assimilate the data collected and interpolate values for the many locations not monitored, and an internet portal to convey the information to users. If a National Water Census is to be implemented, some of the next steps for the water availability and use component may be found in a 2002 Report to Congress, **"Concepts for a National Assessment of Water Availability and Use" (U.S. Geological** Survey, 2002). The Census will also include water quality monitoring so that managers are aware of times and places where water quality is degraded and unable to sustain its intended uses. The Census will permit estimates of the movement of pollutants from watersheds to their downstream river reaches, lakes, reservoirs, estuaries, and the coastal zone. The benefits of a National Water Census will accrue through a combination of monitoring networks integrated with models to estimate water-quality conditions at those places not monitored.

Mt. Rainier, Washington. Snowmelt in the west provides water for crops and cities.

HYDROLOGIC APPLICATIONS OF MICROGRAVITY MEASUREMENTS: MEASURING CHANGES IN GROUND-WATER STORAGE

Ground water is stored within the pore spaces of aquifers. Monitoring changes in the amount of water stored in aquifers once required costly measurement and analysis of changing ground-water levels at numerous wells. Now, the National Aeronautical and Space Administration (NASA) and the U.S. Geological Survey (USGS) are using space-based and land-based gravity methods, respectively, to measure changes in ground-water storage. These methods apply Newton's law of gravity—the acceleration of gravity is directly proportional to mass. As an aquifer is drained by pumpage or filled by recharge, its mass changes, which results in changes in the strength of the gravitational field. Repeated measurements of the gravitational field from space or at a network of terrestrial stations are compared to produce gravity change across a study area. The gravity change is integrated to estimate total change in mass and ground-water storage.

The NASA Gravity Recovery and Climate Experiment (GRACE) measures change in ground water on a regional and subcontinental scale. Two co-orbiting satellites completely map the Earth's gravity field on a monthly basis with an accuracy of better than a μGal (one part per billion of the Earth's gravity).

The USGS is using repeat microgravity surveys in several drainage basins to better define ground-water budgets and estimate specific yield of the aquifer. Recent technological advances in geophysical techniques have made measurement of the extremely small gravitational changes caused by fluctuations of water volume practical. An aquifer's specific yield can be estimated if measured water-level data are available for correlation. Results from a micro- gravity study in southern Arizona showed that storage change ranged from a 66,000 acre-feet accretion in 1989-99, an El Niño year, to a 268,000 acre-feet depletion in 2000-2001. Hence the importance of systematically monitoring storage change, when one year may account for most of the recharge that occurs over many years.

Other agencies cooperating to develop these methods include the National Oceanic and Atmospheric Administration's National Geodetic Survey, who use precise gravity for geodetic control, the National Science

Foundation, and the Pima County, Arizona Department of Transportation and Flood Control District.

Time-differenced microgravity measurements have the potential to provide water managers of the future with answers to questions about changes in water storage, which will be crucial to making informed decisions about water use and conservation. Other uses for this technology include evaluating new methods for artificially recharging ground water and evaluating the effect of climate change on groundwater storage.

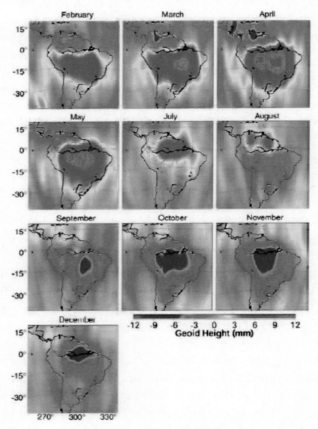

GRACE data measured the weight of as much as 10 centimeters (4 inches) of ground-water accumulations from heavy tropical rains, particularly in the Amazon basin (shown here) and Southeast Asia. Red color shows increased gravity resulting from ground-water storage. Smaller signals caused by changes in ocean circulation were also visible.

The Subcommittee on Water Availability and Quality has identified the following critical actions to implement a National Water Census:

- A national water quality monitoring network has been designed by the National Water Quality Monitoring Council. This is an important component of a National Water Census; the census of water resources will complement and coordinate with the Council's monitoring principles and design.
- In partnership with State, regional, and local water agencies, devise an interagency national strategy for conducting a National Water Census; that is, a periodic inventory of the quantity and quality of the nation's (1) water resources (surface-water, ground-water, and snow resources), (2) water use, and (3) water infrastructure.
- Develop and adopt data collection, data communication, and data availability standards and protocols for nationwide (1) water resources, (2) water use, and (3) water infrastructure.
- Integrate existing monitoring networks to provide nationally uniform (1) surface and ground-water and snow data, (2) water-use data, and (3) infrastructure data.
- Develop a strategy to establish regional and national priorities for the highest level needs for (1) surface- and ground-water and snow monitoring, (2) water use, and (3) water infrastructure monitoring in the United States.

Develop a New Generation of Water Monitoring Techniques

The monitoring of water quantity and quality is ripe for technological innovations that hold the promise of more comprehensive, accurate, and timely data at a cost savings compared to current labor-intensive methods. A new generation of water monitoring techniques will transform the way we monitor the quantity and quality of water in a river, lake, aquifer, wetland, estuary, snowpack, soil, and the atmosphere and improve measurement of the amounts of water withdrawn, consumed, and returned by various human activities. Cost effective, precise, and timely monitoring is especially important when health and property are at risk during floods, droughts, and accidental or deliberate contamination of source waters. Rapid detection of pathogens in recreational waters should reduce the occurrence of unnecessary, inconvenient, and expensive beach closures, and rapid detection of contaminant plumes in rivers should save lives and dollars by protecting drinking-water intakes. Many different monitoring technologies are promising for these purposes, including new in-situ sensors for chemical, biological, and radiological contaminants, time-differential gravity measurements to determine aquifer storage (see textbox, "Hydrologic applications of microgravity measurements"); microbial source tracking to determine the source of pathogens in recreational and drinking water (see textbox, "Microbial source tracking to identify the source of fecal contamination"); hydroacoustics to measure water velocity and sediment transport; remote sensing of quantity and quality (currently effective at regional or continental scales); and nanotechnology for use in a variety of rapid analytical methods.

New water-monitoring methods have significant potential for development of world markets. Biotechnology is particularly promising in the face of an ever- increasing level of concern about worldwide movements of pathogens that are spread by domestic and wild populations of animals. Development of new water-monitoring technologies helps maintain American preeminence in water science and technology, and strengthens our economy. The businesses involved in this field have a strong export market—the world looks to the United States for advancement in water monitoring and other nations want to use the technologies used by U.S. government agencies. Also, significant savings will be achieved if we revolutionize the way that water data are collected. Even with the advent of sophisticated sensors, solid-state data storage devices, and satellite telemetry, there is still a large human labor component in monitoring systems, with high costs associated with bringing technicians to a field site to calibrate and service equipment and collect samples.

The next generation U.S. weather monitoring satellites are scheduled to begin orbiting in 2012.

MICROBIAL SOURCE TRACKING TO IDENTIFY THE SOURCE OF FECAL CONTAMINATION

Many of the Nation's resource waters fail to achieve sanitary water-quality standards as required by the Clean Water Act, and public health is at risk from exposure to water contaminated by human or animal fecal matter. Water-resource managers need a scientific basis by which to provide good stewardship over water resources. Microbial Source Tracking (MST) refers to a group of tools now under development by the scientific community to distinguish among different sources of fecal contamination. The U.S. Environmental Protection Agency, U.S. Geological Survey, National Oceanic and Atmospheric Administration, and U.S. Department of Agriculture are working together to develop and test a set of tools that range from detection of antibiotic resistance profiles and genetic "fingerprints" of individual isolates to probing whole-water nucleic acid extracts for the presence of source-specific pathogens (such as *Cryptosporidium* and various viruses) or other genetic markers.

Significant progress has been made, but none of the currently available tools is completely accurate, nor is any one tool universally applicable to all objectives. To attain the potential of MST, several key components are being addressed, including:

- Further development of methods to rapidly and quantitatively recover DNA and RNA from water samples
- Further development of methods to rapidly and quantitatively detect markers in extracts by quantitative polymerase chain reaction, microarrays, and other new methods
- Consistent and comprehensive characterization of marker occurrence and distribution among host populations
- Identification and characterization of novel host-specific markers

Federal agencies are working toward the day when MST will indicate specific sources of fecal contamination to drinking water sources. This will give managers the tools needed to target regulations and investments to most effectively reduce *E. coli* and enterococci counts to meet recreational-water quality standards, and support requirements for development of Total Maximum Daily Load plans to comply with water-quality health standards. In addition, identification of fecal sources is relevant to source-water protection programs and to the development of accurate microbial risk assessment models.

Stoeckel, D.M., 2005, Selection and application of microbial source tracking tools for water-quality investigations: U.S. Geological Survey Techniques and Methods 2-A3, 43 p.
Santo Domingo, J.W., 2005, Microbial source tracking guide document: Environmental Protection Agency report 600-R-05-064, 135 p.

A consortium of Federal agencies engaged in water monitoring will prioritize and plan implementation of specific improvements to water monitoring science and technology. For example, agencies that currently track the source of pathogens will work together to take recent advancements in genomic research and use them to help ensure safety in recreational waters.

The Subcommittee on Water Availability and Quality has identified the following critical actions to develop a new generation of water monitoring technology:

- Develop sensors and measurement systems to remotely measure water volumes and movement—inexpensively, precisely, and in real time—in rivers, lakes, aquifers, wetlands, estuaries, snowpack, and soil.
- Develop sensors and systems to measure water quality inexpensively in real time.
- Develop and adopt data collection, data communication, and data availability standards and protocols for new monitoring technologies.

Develop and Expand Technologies for Enhancing Reliable Water Supply

As traditional water supplies in streams and fresh-water aquifers become allocated to users, new supplies of water from marginal or impaired sources, such as industrial and municipal wastewater, produced water from oil and gas extraction, brackish water, and other waters, should be identified and developed (see textbox, "Water extracted with the production of oil and gas"). The United States will expand technologies for enhancing reliable water supplies and will widen the range of options for delivering water to growing populations. These technologies include desalination, water treatment and reuse, and more efficient methods of water use in the agriculture, energy, buildings, and industry sectors. Federal agencies will work with others to develop these technologies and obtain objective data on costs and efficiencies of leading treatment and storage technologies. This information will include data on the extent to which these technologies remove low-level contamination (dissolved solids, metals, pharmaceuticals, pesticides, and other organic chemicals), on the energy efficiency of the technologies, and on the water efficiency of the technologies (for example, how much of the water withdrawn or stored will actually be available for use). These new technologies will not only enhance water-supply options domestically but will enhance U.S. competitiveness in the global market for new water infrastructure technology in developing nations.

A critical factor in expanding the availability of fresh water is storage. The ability of water managers to store water during times of abundance and to recover that water during times of need will greatly improve the efficient use of available water resources. Science and technology will help us improve artificial recharge technologies and reduce their adverse impacts.

The Subcommittee on Water Availability and Quality has identified the following critical actions to provide the tools necessary to enhance reliable water supply:

- Identify and pursue appropriate Federal research opportunities for improving and expanding technologies for enhanced use of marginal or impaired water supplies. Such technologies might be applied to desalination, water treatment and reuse, or conservation in the United States and other countries.

An extension specialist examines a purple pipe used for wastewater irrigation.

- Develop technologies and provide scientific information to inform strategies for expanding water storage and recovery in aquifers, including improving understanding of source water and aquifer characteristics and response during cycles of injection and withdrawal.

Develop Innovative Water-Use Technologies and Tools to Enhance Their Public Acceptance

Innovative technologies for expanding water supply and changing the ways in which water is used may be viewed unfavorably by the consuming public. The point has to be made that doing nothing also imposes costs, both for consumers and the economy. Water managers should rely on behavioral research that suggests the best approaches for encouraging the public, industry, and agriculture to be water-efficient and have low environmental impact. These new approaches will include adoption of low-impact landscape designs, water-efficient appliances and water reuse systems for irrigation of urban lands or for waste disposal. New agricultural practices will include irrigation that minimizes long-term water consumption per unit of crop output and innovative methods for managing nutrients, insects, weeds, and soil losses. Industrial innovations will include reuse of water and recycling of heat and chemicals. Thermoelectric generation will benefit from developing advanced water-treatment technologies that would allow use of impaired water for cooling as well as from developing advanced cooling technologies.

In addition to understanding and applying the educational, regulatory, or economic measures that encourage adoption of these methods and technologies, water managers will anticipate possible resistance by water users who are accustomed to unlimited cheap water. With strong public acceptance of new methods for increasing efficiency of water use, the costs building new water-delivery, storage, and treatment systems will be reduced, and negative impacts on water resources will be minimized.

Social, behavioral, and economic science research will predict how communities, agricultural users, and industrial users will respond to the implementation of new, unconventional practices. In addition, social scientists will help water managers anticipate cultural and behavioral changes that may occur as a result of environmental changes or other broad changes arising from climate variability and change. Social sciences will provide tools for predicting how governmental incentives and market incentives might be used to influence and optimize water use.

WATER EXTRACTED WITH THE PRODUCTION OF OIL AND GAS

Water is commonly abundant in rocks that host accumulations of oil and gas. As a consequence of this association, a significant volume of water is extracted with the production of crude oil, natural gas, and coalbed methane. This is referred to as produced water. The Department of Energy's National Energy Technology Laboratory predicts that produced waters from all sources in the contiguous 48 States will total approximately 20 billion barrels (840 billion gallons) in 2025. The quantity and quality of this "produced water" at any given location, in addition to economic and legal factors, determines whether this is a useful resource or wastewater. In general, most coalbed methane water is of better quality than water produced from conventional oil and gas wells.

Water produced with coalbed methane extraction usually contains sodium, bicarbonate, and chloride. Coalbed methane waters are relatively low in sulfate because the chemical conditions in coalbeds favor the conversion of sulfate to sulfide; sulfide is removed as a gas or precipitate. The total dissolved solids of coal-bed methane water ranges from 200 milligrams per liter (mg/L) to 170,000 mg/L (for comparison, the recommended total dissolved solids limit for potable water is 500 mg/L, for irrigation, 1,000-2,000 mg/L; seawater averages 35,000 mg/L total dissolved solids).

Ongoing studies provide information on the composition and volumes of coalbed methane water in some of the Nation's most active areas of production. Researchers from the U.S. Geological Survey (USGS), Bureau of Land Management, Bureau of Indian Affairs, State agencies, and private companies are cooperating in an effort to provide a better understanding of coalbed methane resources and associated water. The Produced Waters Database (http://energy first compiled by the Department of Energy Fossil Energy Research Center and since updated by the USGS, provides the location, geologic setting, sample type, and major ion composition of produced waters.

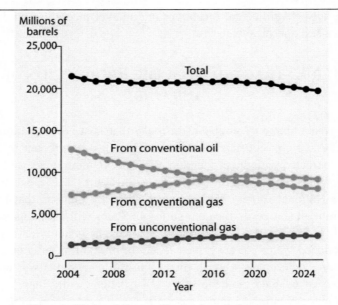

Department of Energy National Energy Technology Laboratory,
http://www.netl.doe.gov/technologies/oil-gas/publications/AP/Program063.pdf]

Forecast of produced water in the onshore 48 contiguous states. Unconventional
gas sources include coalbed methane, gas shales, and tight sands.

In one study of the local effects of produced water, targeting part of the
Powder River Basin in Wyoming and Montana, the USGS is cooperating
with the Wyoming Department of Environmental Quality to monitor real-
time water quality to determine produced water's suitability for use in
irrigation. Currently, most produced water in this area is discharged to
constructed reservoirs or into surface drainages, where it may infiltrate into
the ground, become part of the streamflow, or evaporate. Real-time data on
surface-water   quality   data   are   available   at   http://
waterdata.usgs.gov/wy/nwis/current/?type=quality (see Powder River at
Sussex, Wyoming; Crazy Woman Creek near Arvada, Wyoming; Clear
Creek near Arvada, Wyoming; and Powder River at Moorhead, Montana).
Readily available continuous, real-time water-quality data gives local
irrigators a critical tool for decisionmaking.

Clear Creek in the Powder River Basin, Wyoming

Water-quality sampling at Powder River

Clark, M.L., and Mason, J.P., 2006, Water-quality characteristics, including sodium-adsorption ratios, for four sites in the Power River Drainage Basin, Wyoming and Montana, water years 2001-2004: U.S. Geological Survey Scientific Investigations Report 2006-5113, 22 p.

Department of Energy National Energy Technology Laboratory, Produced water from oil and natural gas operations—setting the context: (http://www.netl.doe.gov/technologies/oil-gas/publications/AP/ Program063.pdf).

Rice, C.A., and Nuccio, V., 2000, Water produced with coalbed methane: U.S. Geological Survey Fact Sheet FS-156-00, 2 p.

Social, behavioral, economic, and management research will be applied to reduce conflict and better manage competing demands on our water resources and to develop ways to better incorporate scientific and technical information into risk management and water-resource decisionmaking. The social and behavioral sciences will also inform efforts to improve public awareness and education, to facilitate technology transfer, and to apply the legal and economic tools that affect water use.

Successful regulatory reform of water laws and practices associated with intro-ducing new technologies and new analytical methods will depend on public and legislative understanding of the societal benefits to be derived from these changes.

The Subcommittee on Water Availability and Quality has identified the following critical actions for appropriate agencies to develop innovative water-use technologies and attain public acceptance of them:

- Develop innovative technologies to use water more efficiently in the agricultural, energy, buildings, and industry sectors.
- Increase and improve research in the social, behavioral, and economic sciences to provide the understanding and tools to deal with the human impacts of changing water availability and use in the United States.
- Increase investment in public education and outreach at all levels dealing with issues of water availability, water quality, and water use.

Develop Collaborative Tools and Processes for Water Infrastructure Solutions

Finding scientific and technical solutions to problems of water availability and quality will require extensive cooperation and collaboration among Federal, State, and local agencies, private sector water experts, stakeholders, and the public (see textbox, "Collaborating to maintain flood control and improve riverine ecosystems"). Collaboration will be particularly important in identifying and addressing infrastructure problems and needs. The Nation's water infrastructure needs and solutions will be studied and addressed in a manner integrating physical and social sciences. Federal research in both the physical and social sciences will help develop and test innovative collaborative tools and methods, including public participation/collaboration processes, decision-support computer technologies, and techniques for integrating these within various contexts. Tools may include portable, physical/social simulation modules, software to link existing water management software, and interfaces for both collaborative model development and displaying modeling results and tradeoffs. Processes may include collaborative process design (for example, how to engage different stakeholders during different parts of the planning and decisionmaking process, meeting formats, and structures), conflict assessment and resolution techniques, and decisionmaking methods. This effort will draw on existing initiatives with Federal and non-Federal partners. Integrating traditional engineering design with ecosystems science will lead to complementary, innovative water infrastructure designs that enhance nutrient recycling, flood mitigation, aquifer recharge, and stormwater management.

The Subcommittee on Water Availability and Quality has identified the following critical actions by appropriate agencies to develop collaborative tools and processes for U.S. water solutions:

- Develop an interagency research program for collaborative decisionmaking in a wide variety of water infrastructure and use applications.
- Initiate pilot studies to integrate emerging decision tools with stakeholder input and new data sources to improve quality and ownership of water management decisions.

Navigation lock and dam on Allegheny River, Pennsylvania

COLLABORATING TO MAINTAIN FLOOD CONTROL AND IMPROVE RIVERINE ECOSYSTEMS

Like all rivers, Kentucky's Green River serves multiple, sometimes competing, interests. Green River provides habitat for 151 species of fish and 71 species of fresh-water mussels. It provides base-level flow to Mammoth Cave, the world's largest known cave system. The Green River Dam provides flood protection and lake-based recreation. To balance these multiple uses, Federal scientists and engineers instituted a collaborative process to assess the needs of the various water users and to manage the infrastructure to provide win-win solutions.

In 2002 The Nature Conservancy and the U.S. Army Corps of Engineers began the Sustainable Rivers Project, a partnership to restore and preserve rivers across the country while maintaining flood control and human uses of the river system. Learning how flow regulation influences habitat is an ongoing process. The Sustainable Rivers Project is not only using the best science that is currently available to improve the habitat while meeting project mission goals, but is also helping to advance the understanding of the complex interactions of flows and water levels with biological outcomes by collecting important hydrologic and biological data and supporting a wide range of scientists who can document the effect of water management changes. In the Green River, multiple partners, including six universities, six Federal agencies, three State agencies, four counties, two cities, and six conservation/citizen groups have collaboratively developed a new management regime for the dam.

The Green River flows under a bridge near Greensburg, Kentucky, site of a U.S. Geological Survey streamgage. Water willows and mussels are common on or near gravel bars at riffles.

Bottlebrush crayfish, native to Green River, is North America's largest species at 11.5 inches.

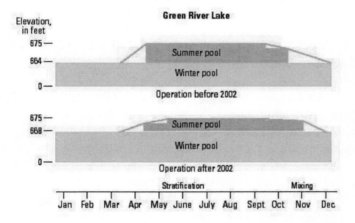

Graph showing changes in the reservoir operation rule that once only protected human life and property but now also benefits aquatic ecosystems.

This collaborative effort has improved habitat in and along the river and identified a more ecologically compatible water-release schedule from Green River Dam. The revised schedule includes delayed fall drawdown, higher winter pool, delayed spring filling, and higher releases during non-crop seasons and after floods or high water peaks have passed. Delaying fall releases until after reservoir mixing (a delay of about 45–60 days) avoids disrupting fall spawning for a number of fishes and mussels and lengthens the recreational boating season. These changes provide significant benefits to plants and animals, while maintaining the dam's primary purpose of flood control and increasing lake recreational benefits.

> Collaboration regarding flood control and riverine ecosystems on the Green River has resulted in the reproduction and recruitment of three endangered species of fresh-water mussels, the near elimination of unseasonable backflows into Mammoth Cave National Park, and extension of the recreation season on Green River Lake.
>
> Turner, W. M. and Byron, W. J., 2006, Green River Lake; pilot project for sustainable rivers, 2006: ASCE Operations Management Conference— Operating Reservoirs in Changing Conditions, Sacramento, California, August 14–16, 2006.
> U.S. Army Corps of Engineers, Louisville District, March 2006, Environmental assessment and finding of no significant impact, Pool re-regulation, Green River Lake, Kentucky.

Improve Understanding of Water-Related Ecosystem Services and Ecosystem Needs for Water

Despite the progress that has been made in the field of ecohydrology, considerable uncertainty remains about water-related ecosystem services and water requirements to maintain these services. The science has evolved from one that simply indicated what minimum flows might be needed to maintain a particular species in a river. Today we recognize that the timing and magnitude of flow and the physical and chemical quality of water are also essential factors for maintaining productive and viable aquatic systems (see textbox: "Collaborating to maintain flood control and improve riverine ecosystems"). Furthermore, we know that ecosystems play a role in cleaning and storing water, but we have not yet quantified the water-related ecosystem services. Research needs include quantifying important processes and services provided by functioning ecosystems, such as recycling of nutrients, infiltration of stormwater, maintenance of base- flow, aquifer recharge, sediment transport, flood mitigation, and maintenance of productive aquatic and riparian habitat. Research is also needed to document ecological responses to flow variability and water quality conditions. In addition, we need to develop an array of analytical and decision-support tools so that we can describe and predict ecological and social consequences of water management decisions. We need to develop an interdisciplinary program of research to develop innovative ways to identify, characterize, and quantify societal, ecologic, and economic attributes of water management decisions, as well as the means to effectively convey these attributes to the public and to decisionmakers.

The Subcommittee on Water Availability and Quality has identified the following critical actions by appropriate agencies to address the need to improve understanding of the needs and benefits of ecosystems in U.S. water systems:

- Work with Federal and non-Federal partners to establish or expand ecosystem monitoring to address watershed or region-specific water needs as well as provisions of ecosystems.
- Expand ecosystem research programs to include hydrologic variables in ecosystems-based studies.

Improve Predictive Hydrologic Models and Their Applications

Because water management decisions are made over a range of geographic and time scales, Federal research on hydrologic modeling must integrate across time and spatial scales. Currently, different hydrologic models are used by water-science and operational agencies to guide water managers in making hourly to seasonal decisions about water storage, water delivery, and drought and flood risk. Yet too frequently different data structures and conventions prevent inter-model comparisons and the linkage of multiple models for multidisciplinary projects and data sharing. Furthermore, water managers are calling for improved and usable forecasting and prediction models for individual watersheds.

Development of common data structures and conventions will allow for integrated, robust hydrologic forecasts while maintaining user-specific applications across different time and spatial scales. Hydrologic forecasts will also need to consider long-term water availability, combining watershed-scale hydrologic process models with regional aquifer system models and global and regional- scale atmospheric and climate models. Water managers and decisionmakers require existing and forecasted information that accounts for the roles of natural vegetation, irrigated land, ground-water development, and urban impervious surfaces on the long-term water budget. In addition, hydrologic models and operational forecast systems will be successful and accurate over long periods of time only if they consider the effects of climate variability and change on water availability and quality. Creating new multidisciplinary models will depend on the convergence of data and theory from the fields of hydrology, ecology, and atmospheric sciences.

Over 200,000 acres of water provide ideal habitat for wildlife on USACE land in Tennessee and Kentucky.

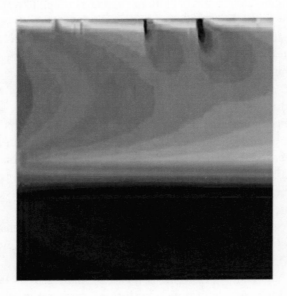

Hydrologic modeling image showing fraction soil water content in the Washita River Basin, Oklahoma

To maximize the utility of hydrologic and ecologic forecasts for water management, linkages between Federal, State, and local agencies should be improved. This will be accomplished through the development of a "community hydrologic prediction system." Adoption of this community system will infuse the science of new models so that advancements will be expanded to different applications and enable the shared use of models in hydrologic forecast operations. Data sets will also be linked and shared through this community system. The private sector will be included in data collection and dissemination, forecasting simulations, and water resource management activities.

Comprehensive water models will be useful to evaluate alternative conservation measures and new technologies, innovative storage techniques, land-use practices, flood frequency, amount of base flow during dry periods, and the effects of reservoir, channel, and port sedimentation. Pilot studies of management practices, coupled with integrated models of ground water, surface water, and biological systems are needed to confirm scientific theories and to translate proposed land-use practices into estimates of resultant water quantity and quality and ecosystem health.

Elements of these are already being incorporated in the activities of a number of Federal agencies through collaborative efforts. One example is the Interagency Steering Committee on Multimedia Environmental Models, which is introducing common standards for a variety of modeling approaches.

A researcher monitors water-level data and models ground water flow.

In addition to purely hydrologic modeling, institutional models and forecast services to improve water management at the watershed and subwatershed (individual field or neighborhood) scale and on a State and regional basis are also needed. These models and services will incorporate accurate representation of water rights, and thus will help water users and water managers to make the best possible longterm water-related investments. Water users will choose how to respond to changes in the available supply through new awareness and knowledge of the resource.

The Subcommittee on Water Availability and Quality has identified the following critical actions by appropriate agencies to address the need for expanding the quality and use of hydrologic models:

- Existing hydrologic models will be strengthened, integrated, and transformed into tools for making decisions on watershed and subwatershed scales.
- Hydrologic models will, to the extent possible, be linked to climate models that simulate the water cycle over broad geographic areas and long time periods.
- Hydrologic models will be coupled with institutional models to provide a full suite of physical, economic, and technological decision tools for water managers.
- Advanced hydrologic models will be transitioned to operational services through establishment of a "community hydrologic prediction system."

The Missouri River separates agriculture from the city life as it flows past Jefferson City, Missouri.

NEXT STEPS

The Subcommittee on Water Availability and Quality (SWAQ) has already begun follow-on planning to implement the strategic elements identified in this report. In planning implementation for these priority topics, SWAQ will emphasize topics where current or historical collaboration in science and technology has led to better outcomes as well as key areas in need of enhanced collaboration.

For a given priority implementation, SWAQ will convene a multiagency team to review the needs within these areas and benchmark skills, capabilities, and tools currently available within appropriate Federal agencies to meet these needs. The teams will recommend pathways to improve current capabilities to meet our emerging and future needs. Those pathways will be pursued through coordination of agency planning and budget processes, and through coordination with the Office of Management and Budget. This will ensure the best use of current capabilities and past investments, and ensure that future investments are efficient, coordinated, and avoid duplication.

CONCLUSION

The status of the Nation's water resources will continue to change with growing population, increasing urbanization, changing industrial and agricultural practices, and changing climate. Science can inform us about the status of our water resources and help us anticipate the likely effects of water-policy and management practices on those resources.

Authority to manage water resources is largely delegated to States, Tribes, and local municipalities. SWAQ is committed to productive collaboration with these water resource managers. SWAQ has identified a Federal role that emphasizes the variety of ways that water science and technology can be used to inform policies and decisions for managing water resources for the public good. The water science and technology portfolio identified by SWAQ encompasses research that produces near-term results as well as anticipating future water issues. This research includes creating and disseminating fundamental knowledge on water resources and developing new technologies to support informed choices for protecting and expanding water resource availability. This research will be carried out in collaboration with State and local governments, Tribes, the private sector, universities and other educational institutions, and other stakeholders.

In the future, water managers will need to update policies and practices to respond to changing water resource conditions and to reflect new knowledge. Our goal is to identify strategic Federal investments in water science and technology that will yield results useful for creating new and flexible management solutions. The successful stewardship of the Nation's water resources requires that science and engineering meet the needs of water managers, that water managers are able to act on new information, and that scientists, engineers, and managers work together to maintain our vital water resources.

SELECTED BIBLIOGRAPHY

National Research Council, (1997). *Building a foundation for sound environmental decisions*: Washington, D.C., National Academy Press, 87 p.

National Research Council, (2001). *Envisioning the agenda for water resources research in the twenty-first century*: Washington, D.C., National Academies Press, 61 p.

National Research Council, (2002). *Estimating water use in the United States; a new paradigm for the National Water-Use Information Program*: Washington, D.C., National Academies Press, 176 p.

National Research Council, (2004a). *Assessing the National Streamflow Information Program*: Washington, D.C., National Academies Press, 164 p.

National Research Council, (2004b). *Confronting the Nation's water problems; the role of research*: Washington, D.C., National Academies Press, 310 p.

National Science and Technology Council, *Committee on Environment and Natural Resources, Subcommittee on Water Availability and Quality*, (2004). Science and technology to support fresh water availability in the United States, 19 p.

U.S. General Accounting Office, (July 2003). *Freshwater supply; States' views of how Federal agencies could help them meet the challenges of expected shortages*: GAO-03-514.

U.S. General Accounting Office, (June 2004). *Watershed management; better coordination of data collection efforts needed to support key decisions*: GAO- 04-382.

U.S. Geological Survey, (2002). *Report to Congress—Concepts for national assessment of water availability and use*: U.S. Geological Survey Circular 1223, 34 p.

U.S. Government Accountability Office, (March 2005). *Freshwater programs; Federal agencies funding in the United States and abroad*: GAO-05-253.

APPENDIX I. FEDERAL AGENCIES' ROLE IN THE SCIENCE AND TECHNOLOGY OF WATER AVAILABILITY AND QUALITY

Department of Agriculture—Agricultural Research Service (ARS)

The Agricultural Research Service (ARS) is the U.S. Department of Agriculture's principal intramural scientific research agency. The agency's research and technology transfer efforts related to water availability and quality are carried out by scientists and engineers through a coordinated system of nationally distributed Research Centers. The mission of our water-related research is to conduct fundamental and applied research on the processes that control water availability and quality for the health and economic growth of the American people, and develop new and improved technologies for managing the Nation's agricultural water resources. These advances in knowledge and technologies will provide producers, action agencies, local communities, and resource advisors with the conservation practices, tools, models, and decision support systems they need to improve water conservation and water use efficiency in agriculture, enhance water quality, protect rural and urban communities from the ravages of droughts and floods, improve agricultural and urban watersheds, and prevent the degradation of riparian areas, wetlands, and stream corridors.

Department of Agriculture—Cooperative State Research, Education, and Extension Service (CSREES)

The Cooperative State Research, Education, and Extension Service (CSREES) Water Program provides Federal financial assistance to universities, private industries, non-profit organizations, and individuals to create and disseminate knowledge for improving or protecting water resources. CSREES funds research, education, and extension activities that help to ensure a safe and reliable source of water that meets the need for food, fiber, and energy production; human health, use, and economic growth; and to maintain and protect ecosystems. **CSREES' unique niche is funding** research, education, and extension programs that work to protect and improve water resources in agricultural, rural, and urbanizing watersheds, including forest lands, rangelands, and croplands. Basic research programs develop new knowledge related to water quality impairments and water supply or scarcity and new management and technology tools needed to address these issues. Integrated research, education, and extension programs create and disseminate knowledge needed to resolve stakeholder (farmer, rancher, and homeowner) identified water-resource issues at the watershed scale.

Department of Agriculture—Economic Research Service (ERS)

The Economic Research Service (ERS) is the main source of economic information and research from the U.S. Department of Agriculture (USDA). ERS brings the perspective of economic analysis to critical issues confronting farmers, agribusiness, consumers, and policymakers. **The agency's analysis** informs public and private decisionmakers on issues of agriculture, food, the environment, and rural America. ERS research addresses how the quantity and quality of water supplies available to agriculture affect food production and profits. Survey data are used to monitor the use of water as an input to agricultural production and to assess the adoption of irrigation technologies. ERS assesses the policies and economic incentives that affect technology choices and the impact of those choices on environmental quality, including the quality of water for human and wildlife uses.

Department of Agriculture—Natural Resources Conservation Service (NRCS)

The Natural Resources Conservation Service (NRCS) is the primary Federal agency that works with private landowners to help them conserve, maintain and improve their natural resources. The agency emphasizes voluntary, science- based conservation; technical assistance; partnerships; incentive-based programs; and cooperative problem solving at the community level. Agency science and technology efforts related to water availability and quality are carried out by scientists and engineers in a variety of National Centers. Responsibilities include providing water supply forecasts, water and climate analysis, information, and services for NRCS, partners, and customers; providing emergency support to customers in response to extreme natural resource events; and operating the Snowpack Telemetry (SNOTEL) data collection system for the United States and the Soil Climate Analysis Network (SCAN). This agency also provides technical leadership, guidance, support, and expertise for water resources planning, including watershed restoration efforts. Watershed restoration encompasses watershed protection, rehabilitation, flood prevention projects, and river basin studies, including flood plain management studies and program neutral planning.

Department of Agriculture—Forest Service (FS)

The mission of the USDA Forest Service is to sustain the health, diversity, and productivity of the Nation's forests and grasslands. The agency implements water programs through the Research and Development (R&D), National Forest System, and State and Private Forestry programs to provide clean and reliable sources of water. The research focus is to understand the effects of forest and rangeland management practices and related human and natural disturbances on water quantity, quality and the sustainability of watershed functions. Forest Service R&D provides scientific understanding to distinguish healthy from degraded watersheds and to provide the technical basis for restoration to functioning, healthy, and sustainable condition. Forest Service R&D long-term experimental watershed studies are key to understanding how healthy watersheds function and what processes enhance or impair the quantity and quality of water that comes from forests. Forest Service scientists work closely with resource managers to synthesize research results, provide technology, and deliver the information to develop, adapt and evaluate management approaches.

Department of Commerce—National Oceanic and Atmospheric Administration (NOAA)

The National Oceanic and Atmospheric Administration (NOAA) delivers water information and predictions affecting all hydroclimatic conditions from floods to droughts. This includes high-resolution analyses of snow pack, precipitation, and soil conditions, and the nationally consistent production of water supply estimates, stream flow forecasts, and flood warnings that save lives and conserve America's water resources. NOAA's information products extend to climate, ecosystems, and commerce as well. Within NOAA, the National Weather Service (NWS) delivers flood watches, river and flash flood warnings, and river and lake level forecasts through 122 Weather Forecast Offices to a broad spectrum of customers, including emergency and water resource managers. Emergency managers use these forecasts for both strategic, long-term, and tactical, short-term planning. Weather Forecast Offices receive river, lake level and flash flood guidance from 13 watershed-based River Forecast Centers. These Centers also provide river forecasts to water resource managers. NOAA also supports research to improve climate prediction for hydrological applications and the use of information on climate variability and change by water resource managers. These water resource managers make critical decisions that affect flood control, water supply, water quality, river and lake transportation, irrigation, hydropower, and recreation and maintain the ecological health of the rivers.

Department of Defense—U.S. Army Corps of Engineers (USACE)

The Corps (USACE) serves the Armed Forces and the Nation by providing vital engineering services and capabilities, as a public service, across the full spectrum of operations—from peace to war—in support of national interests. USACE supports the Nation's interests by building broad-based relationships and alliances to collaboratively provide comprehensive, systems-based, sustainable and integrated solutions to national and international water-resources challenges. The Corps is proud to have the responsibility of helping to care for these important aquatic resources. Through its Civil Works program the Corps carries out a wide array of projects that provide coastal protection, flood protection, hydropower, navigable waters and ports, recreational opportunities, and water supply. The Corps' environmental mission has two major focus areas: restoration and stewardship. Efforts in both areas are guided by the Corps' environmental operating principles, which help us balance economic and environmental concerns. Science and technology research on water availability and quality focuses on flood damage reduction, navigation, and environmental business areas.

Department of Energy—Office of Energy Efficiency and Renewable Energy, Office of Science, Office of Fossil Energy, Office of Nuclear Energy, and Office of Environmental Management

The Department of Energy has a variety of energy-water-related activities with national laboratories, universities, and industry. The Office of Fossil Energy conducts research and development on Integrated Gasification Combined Cycle technology, which reduces the water needed to generate power from coal. The Office of Nuclear Energy conducts research and development on water issues for nuclear reactors. The Office of Energy Efficiency and Renewable Energy does research and development and supports deployment of technologies to reduce the use of water in the building and industrial sectors, to reduce the amount of energy used to supply water, and to make use of renewables for water supply. The Office of Science conducts research in basic science, which can lead to breakthrough technologies such as improved membranes for purifying water. The Office of Environmental Management does extensive work in ground-water transport issues to enable better ground-water cleanup technologies.

Department of Health and Human Services—Indian Health Service (IHS)

The Sanitation Facilities Construction Program is the environmental engineering component of the Indian Health Service health delivery system. The Sanitation Facilities Construction Program provides technical and financial assistance related to safe water, wastewater, and solid waste systems. In particular, the Program provides the following services:

- Develops and maintains an inventory of sanitation deficiencies in Indian communities
- Provides engineering assistance with utility master planning and sanitary surveys
- Develops multiagency-funded sanitation projects, assists with grant applications, and leverages of IHS funds
- Provides funding for water supply and waste disposal facilities
- Provides engineering design and/or construction services for water supply and waste disposal facilities
- Provides technical consultation and training for the operation and maintenance of tribally owned water supply and waste disposal systems
- Advocates for Tribes during the development of policies, regulations, and programs
- Assists Tribes with sanitation facility emergencies

Department of Health and Human Services—National Institute of Environmental Health Sciences (NIEHS)

The mission of the NIEHS is to prevent disease and improve human health by using environmental sciences to understand human biology and human disease. Reductions in the quality and availability of water for consumption and recreation is a major worldwide health concern. Research supported by NIEHS is critical to understanding health risks associated with exposure to water contaminants such as toxins from algal blooms, metals such as mercury, and manmade compounds such as pesticides. NIEHS supports its overall mission through extramural research and training grants and contracts that fund work by scientists, environmental health professionals, and other groups worldwide; through intramural research conducted by scientists at the NIEHS facility and in partnership with scientists at universities and hospitals; through toxicological testing and test validation by the National Toxicology Program; and through outreach and communications programs that provide reliable health information to the public, medical practitioners, and public health professionals. Understanding relations between waterborne pollutants and adverse health outcomes is vitally important for addressing health risks and disease burdens in human populations faced with problems of water quality and availability.

Department of the Interior—Bureau of Reclamation

Reclamation is an agency dealing with the 17 Western States; the agency's mission is to manage, develop, and protect water and related resources in an environmentally and economically sound manner in the interest of the public. Reclamation is the Nation's largest wholesale water supplier and the second largest producer of hydroelectric power in the western United States. Because Reclamation manages such a large water infrastructure in the West, research and development efforts focus on ensuring reliable water supply and delivery under the increasing demands placed on water managers in the rapidly growing West. Reclamation's Science and Technology Program furnishes a full range of solutions for water supply and delivery to Reclamation's water and power managers and their stakeholders. Research and development efforts are typically conducted in collaboration with other Federal and non-Federal entities that have a stake in western water solutions. The program has contributed many of the tools and capabilities in use today by Reclamation and western water managers. The Science and Technology Program's primary focus includes improving water delivery reliability, improving water and power infrastructure reliability and safety, advancing water supply technologies and water efficiency solutions, and improving water operations decision support capabilities. Reclamation also funds external research in desalination technologies with emphases on inland brackish water and on lowering the cost of desalination.

Department of the Interior—U.S. Fish and Wildlife Service (USFWS)

The U.S. Fish and Wildlife Service works with others to conserve, protect, and enhance fish, wildlife, plants, and their habitats for the continuing benefit of the American people. Through its various programs and offices, the USFWS works with landowners and others to conserve threatened and endangered species associated with wetland, riparian and aquatic habitats; assesses how flow modifications or water project operations affect fish and wildlife, and recommends to regulatory agencies measures to minimize harmful effects; partners with landowners and others to restore healthy aquatic communities and their associated wetland, riparian and aquatic habitats; and manages its nearly 100 million acre National Wildlife Refuge System. USFWS has a stake as a resource manager in many aspects of Federal water resource science and technology, particularly as it relates to understanding and ensuring the ecological needs of fish and wildlife.

Department of the Interior—U.S. Geological Survey (USGS)

The USGS provides reliable, impartial information about the Nation's water resources. The information is used by decisionmakers to minimize the loss of life and property resulting from floods, droughts, and land movement; to effectively manage ground-water and surface-water resources for domestic, agricultural, commercial, industrial, recreational, and ecological uses; to protect and enhance water resources for human health, aquatic health, and environmental quality; and to contribute to wise physical and economic development of the Nation's resources for the benefit of present and future generations. Many USGS activities related to water availability and quality are performed in cooperation with State and local governments, other Federal agencies, and Tribes. The USGS collects and disseminates basic hydrologic data, conducts interpretive hydrologic studies, and performs fundamental hydrologic research. For example, the USGS operates and maintains national networks of streamgages and wells; collects and maintains the Nation's water use database; measures and assesses the status and trends of our Nation's water quality; performs reconnaissance of emerging contaminants; and collaborates with other agencies to characterize changing water availability.

Department of the Interior—U.S. National Park Service (NPS)

Water is a critical resource for both ecosystems and visitors in the National Park System; therefore, a core mission of the NPS water resources program is to protect and manage water and water-related park resources. To meet this mission, the NPS needs tactical research and technical assistance to enable parks to address critical water-resource protection and management responsibilities. In partnership with parks and others, the Water Resources Division (WRD) of the National Park Service provides leadership, technical assistance, and funding support for understanding, protecting, and managing water and aquatic resources of the National Park System. The WRD provides its services directly to the parks through a broad range of programs in the areas of surface-water and ground-water hydrology and water quality, water rights, watersheds and wetlands, water-resources management planning, fisheries, aquatic ecology, and marine resources. Through the application of science in a planning, stakeholder negotiation, policy, regulatory, or administrative context, WRD's programs help units of the National Park System succeed in enhancing the overall condition of park water and aquatic resources.

Environmental Protection Agency (EPA)

EPA is responsible for ensuring that drinking water is safe and that watersheds, coastal oceans, and their aquatic ecosystems are protected and restored to provide healthy habitat for fish, plants, and wildlife; to support economic and recreational activities; and to ensure a healthy environment for people. Safe Drinking Water Act programs protect human health through the protection and regulation of water supplies, including compliance activities and financial assistance to municipal water-treatment facilities. Clean Water Act programs protect and restore fresh and coastal waters by setting protective criteria and reducing pollutant loads to water bodies. Additional programs target increases in acreage and functions of wetlands; recreational uses of coastal and freshwater beaches; and reduction of pollution leading to fish consumption advisories. EPA's Global Change Research Program (GCRP) assesses the potential impacts of global change on water quality as precipitation and hydrologic regimes are altered. The primary global change stressors studied are climate change, climate variability, and land use change. EPA's GCRP focuses on both human uses (such as impacts to drinking water and wastewater systems) and on impacts to aquatic plant and animal life.

Understanding the relation between natural systems and the uses of water is critical to implementing these diverse programs. To that end, EPA conducts and promotes research, both in-house and extramurally, to support these monitoring, planning, and conservation activities and to support sound rule-making.

National Aeronautics and Space Administration (NASA)

NASA's mission is to pioneer the future in space exploration, scientific discovery, and aeronautics research. In the realm of scientific discovery, one of NASA's goals is to study the Earth from space to advance scientific understanding and meet societal needs. Specifically with regards to water resources, NASA develops remote sensing systems to measure aspects of the global water cycle, such as precipitation, soil moisture, snow cover, river discharge, ground water, evaporation, water quality, and many others. NASA engages in research activities to infuse these observations into modeling systems, either directly or through data assimilation, to improve our ability to assess the current state of the environment as well as enable enhanced weather forecasting and climate prediction capability. As part of these activities, NASA is improving our understanding of how aspects of the water cycle affect climate change, and how in turn climate change might alter the water cycle, both globally and regionally. Through partnerships with other agencies, NASA seeks to extend the benefits of its science results into management, regulatory, and policymaking systems and practices.

National Science Foundation (NSF)

NSF's overall mission is to promote the progress of science, to advance the national health, prosperity, and welfare; and to secure the national defense. NSF supports fundamental research and education across all fields of science and engineering, except medical sciences. Support is provided to scientists and engineers through limited-term awards, primarily to universities and colleges. Water-related research spans basic studies of water across terrestrial, aquatic, atmospheric, and subsurface systems and processes from watershed to global scales. It includes studies of aquatic ecosystem function and health in natural and built domains as well as investigations into new processes for wastewater treatment and techniques to deal with contaminated surface and ground waters. NSF also supports studies of coupling between human and natural systems, the development of new sensors and sensor networks, and the creation of new cyberinfrastructure tools in support of research.

Tennessee Valley Authority (TVA)

The mission of TVA is to develop and operate the Tennessee River system to improve navigation, minimize flood damage, provide electric power, and promote economic development in the Tennessee Valley region. TVA's ongoing research and technology development efforts are in direct support of energy and environmental issues related to TVA's statutory responsibilities for river, land management and power generation. These include, among others, generation and transmission technologies, environmental impacts and control, renewable resources, and other emerging technologies. Emergency response focuses on natural disasters such as flood and drought events, power system emergencies, hazardous material emergencies, protection of water supplies, and homeland security.

APPENDIX II. INTERFACE OF WATER AVAILABILITY WITH DISASTER REDUCTION

Floods and droughts define the extremes of water availability. Too much water or too little water is devastating to life and property. Flooding is the most frequent of natural disasters. One in three Federal disaster declarations is because of flooding; damages reach $2 billion per year. Drought, on the other hand, affects more people than any other natural disaster; damages to property because of drought average $6-8 billion per year.

To address the science and technology needs for disaster reduction, the National Science and Technology Council's Committee on Environment and Natural Resources has established a sister subcommittee to the Subcommittee on Water Availability and Quality (SWAQ) called the Subcommittee on Disaster Reduction (SDR). The SDR includes many of the same Federal agencies as SWAQ and explicitly considers floods and droughts. The SDR recently prepared a document that identified six Grand Challenges for disaster reduction (note that in the SDR document, the terms disasters and hazards encompass events with both natural and technological origins):

- Provide hazard and disaster information where and when it is needed.
- Understand the natural processes that produce hazards.
- Develop hazard mitigation strategies and technologies.
- Recognize and reduce vulnerability of interdependent critical infrastructure.
- Assess disaster resilience using standard methods.
- Promote risk-wise behavior.

SWAQ recognizes that many of the efforts identified in the present Grand Challenges report for Water Availability and Quality will do double duty to reduce the impact of floods and droughts. Indeed, Federal research under SWAQ's purview is to "understand the processes that control water availability and quality, and to collect and make available the data needed to ensure an adequate water supply for the Nation's future." Many SWAQ actions, therefore, will help meet some of the Grand Challenges identified by the SDR. Accordingly, Federal agencies will view many of the recommendations for research priorities of the two subcommittees as mutually reinforcing, albeit with slightly different focus. Ultimately, most of the activities and research identified by SWAQ will serve to reduce the vulnerability of the Nation to the extremes of the hydrologic cycle and thus reduce impacts of hydrologic-induced disasters.

End Notes

[1] For the purposes of this report, ground water refers to water under the surface of the earth, such as soil moisture or water found in aquifers; surface water refers to water on the surface of the earth, such as rivers, lakes, wetlands, and estuaries.

CHAPTER SOURCES

The following chapters have been previously published:

Chapter 1 – This is an edited, excerpted and augmented edition of a United States Congressional Research Service publication, Report Order Code R40573, dated May 11, 2009.

Chapter 2 – This is an edited, excerpted and augmented edition of a Executive Office of the President of the United States Report of the National Science and Technology Council, Committee on Environment and Natural Resources, Subcommittee on Water Availability and Quality, dated September 2007.

INDEX

D

juveniles, 49

K

Katrina, 20, 35, 48, 49
kelp, 52
Kentucky, 128, 130, 132
King, 87

L

labor, 117, 118
labor-intensive, 117
lakes, 114, 120, 148
land, 4, 9, 16, 17, 19, 29, 30, 41, 45, 46, 50,
    51, 52, 63, 64, 65, 71, 73, 74, 84, 88, 90,
    108, 109, 115, 131, 132, 133, 144, 145,
    147
land use, 9, 16, 17, 41, 45, 46, 50, 51, 71,
    108, 109, 133, 145
landfill, 54
large-scale, 8, 10, 16, 18, 22, 23, 35, 40, 50,
    52, 98
law, 5, 7, 14, 25, 26, 28, 42, 64, 65, 66, 68,
    69, 70, 74, 75, 77, 78, 79, 80, 81, 82, 83,
    84, 89, 97, 115
laws, x, 2, 4, 5, 7, 9, 11, 12, 14, 18, 24, 26,
    31, 39, 42, 44, 51, 53, 68, 75, 84, 111,
    126
legislation, ix, x, xi, 1, 2, 6, 7, 11, 14, 23,
    31, 35, 36, 46, 48, 50, 54, 55, 60, 64, 65,
    66, 67, 68, 77, 79, 81, 82, 83, 89, 98
lettuce, 106
levees, 13, 16, 46, 48, 49, 57, 58, 106
license fee, 61, 62
licenses, 26
licensing, 17, 25, 86
lifespan, 106, 107
limitation, 63, 64, 65, 66
limitations, 65, 89
linkage, 64, 131
links, 51
litigation, 27, 37, 79, 81, 83
loans, 7, 70, 71

local action, 22
local government, 4, 45, 51, 71, 84, 136,
    144
location, 17, 73, 101, 123
long period, 131
losses, 16, 42, 43, 45, 122
Louisiana, 50, 52
low-income, 48
low-level, 121

M

maintenance, 35, 38, 39, 50, 53, 60, 61, 65,
    67, 105, 106, 130, 142
management practices, 111, 133, 135, 139
mandates, 98
manpower, 27, 73
market, 79, 81, 118, 121, 123
market incentives, 123
market value, 81
markets, 107, 109, 118
marshes, 54
measurement, 95, 103, 115, 117, 120
measures, 17, 21, 25, 40, 48, 49, 50, 51, 53,
    58, 115, 122, 133, 144
membership, 29, 30, 85
membranes, 141
mercury, 142
metals, 68, 121, 142
methane, 123, 124, 125
metropolitan area, 16, 17, 99
microgravity, 115, 116, 118
migration, 39
Mississippi, 4, 50, 61, 62, 74
Mississippi River, 50, 61, 62, 74
Missouri, 4, 41, 134
modeling, 41, 43, 111, 127, 131, 132, 133,
    134, 146
models, 110, 111, 113, 114, 120, 131, 133,
    134, 137
modules, 127
moisture, 113, 146, 148
Montana, 124, 125
moratorium, 81
movement, 9, 51, 114, 120, 144

Q

R

S

T